W9-BVR-399

SUPER SEARCHERS
on MERGERS & ACQUISITIONS

The Online Secrets of
TOP CORPORATE RESEARCHERS AND M&A PROS

Jan Davis Tudor
Edited by Reva Basch

CyberAge Books

Information Today, Inc.
Medford, New Jersey

First Printing, 2001

Super Searchers on Mergers & Acquisitions:
The Online Secrets of Top Corporate Researchers and M&A Pros

Copyright © 2001 by Jan Davis Tudor

Super Searchers, Volume VI
A series edited by Reva Basch

All rights reserved. No part of this book may be reproduced in any form or by any electronic or mechanical means, including information storage and retrieval systems, without permission in writing from the publisher, except by a reviewer, who may quote brief passages in a review. Published by CyberAge Books, an imprint of Information Today, Inc., 143 Old Marlton Pike, Medford, New Jersey 08055.

Liability
The opinions of the searchers interviewed are their own and not necessarily those of their employers, the author, editor, or publisher. Information Today, Inc. does not guarantee the accuracy, adequacy, or completeness of any information and is not responsible for any errors or omissions or the results obtained from the use of such information.

Trademarks
Trademarks and service names have been used throughout this book. The names are used with capitalization in the style used by the name claimant. The exception is the use of the trademarked name "LISTSERV." Some of the searchers interviewed used this term generically and their usage has been retained in this book. Rather than insert a trademark notation at each occurrence of the name, the publisher states that all such trademarks are used in an editorial manner without any intent to infringe upon the trademark.

Library of Congress Cataloging-in-Publication Data

Tudor, Jan.
   Super searchers on Mergers & Acquisitions : the online secrets of top corporate researchers and M&A pros / Jan Davis Tudor ; edited by Reva Basch.
      p. cm. – (Super searchers ; v. 6)
   Includes bibliographical references and index.
   ISBN 0-910965-48-X
      1. Consolidation and merger of corporations—Research—
Methodology.2.Electronic information resource searching. I.Title: Super searchers on mergers and acquisitions. II. Basch,Reva. III. Title. IV. Series.

   HD2746.5 .T83 2001
   025.06'33883—dc21

                                                    2001016544

Printed and bound in the United States of America

Publisher: Thomas H. Hogan, Sr.
Editor-in-Chief: John B. Bryans
Managing Editor: Janet M. Spavlik
Copy Editor: Dorothy Pike
Production Manager: M. Heide Dengler
Cover Designer: Jacqueline Walter
Book Designer: Anne Alexander, Kara Mia Jalkowski
Indexer: Sharon Hughes

Dedication

This book is dedicated to all the information professionals
out there who are eager and willing to share their knowledge.

About The Super Searchers Web Page

At the Information Today Web site, you will find *The Super Searchers Web Page*, featuring links to sites mentioned in this book. We will periodically update the page, removing dead links and adding additional sites that may be useful to readers.

The Super Searchers Web Page is made available as a bonus to readers of *Super Searchers on Mergers & Aquisitions* and other books in the Super Searchers series. To access the page, an Internet connection and Web browser are required. Go to:

www.infotoday.com/supersearchers

DISCLAIMER: Neither publisher nor authors make any claim as to the results that may be obtained through the use of *The Super Searchers Web Page* or of any of the Internet resources it references. Neither publisher nor authors will be held liable for any results, or lack thereof, obtained by the use of this page or any of its links, for any third-party charges, or for any hardware, software, or other problems that may occur as a result of using it. *The Super Searchers Web Page* is subject to change or discontinuation without notice at the discretion of the publisher.

Table of Contents

Foreword

The modern wave of mergers and acquisitions (M&A) activity is now in its twentieth year, with no letup in sight. It is a boom of unprecedented proportions and unparalleled length. Its magnitude and longevity signify the importance of M&A as a primary vehicle for businesses to survive in an era of awesome challenges stemming from rapid technological change, unrelenting globalization, and persistent pressures to create value for shareholders.

Two decades of dealmaking have produced some lasting effects. A vast body of knowledge and an almanac of techniques have developed to help practitioners do deals the right way. And a corps of sophisticated professionals has been created to put the lore and the methodology into action.

However, doing M&A has gotten no easier. Competition for good companies has intensified. The whole process has accelerated dramatically, often requiring potential buyers to formulate and submit intelligent bids within 24 to 48 hours if they wish to stay in the game. Meanwhile, criticism has mounted that most deals are neither successful nor value-creating.

In such a highly charged environment, there is a premium on good information. Having a firm handle on the correct data, the most influential trends, and the facts on specific companies enables the wise acquirer to choose the best targets, calculate the optimal prices, assess the competition, and smoothly integrate the acquired company for maximization of value. Ideally, the well-informed company amasses intelligence on a continuous basis. But sometimes the pace is so hectic that even a seemingly complete information bank comes up short, leaving the harried acquirer to obtain the suddenly needed data in a hurry—or fly blind if it can't be found.

That is why *Super Searchers on Mergers & Acquisitions* plugs a gap in any company's information base. Jan Tudor has assembled nothing less than the complete compendium of M&A information sources—ranging from databases to authoritative books on the subject—and how to use them. Its value is incalculable, whether it is used to support ongoing intelligence gathering or to telescope the search for critical information when the decision maker is under the gun.

If information is a key weapon in the M&A competition of the twenty-first century, *Super Searchers on Mergers & Acquisitions* is the pathway to finding the most potent ammunition. It can be used by the corporate dealmaker, the company's advisers, even the researchers and librarians who tend to be information generalists rather than M&A specialists. As the M&A wave continues, the need for good information gets even stronger.

Martin Sikora
Editor, *Mergers & Acquisitions: The Dealmaker's Journal*

Acknowledgments

Without the wonderful participation of the 13 individuals I interviewed—Lisa, Mark, Ed, Rob, Luci, Reed, Bruce, Penny, Bob, Jim, Jack, Steven, and Sylvia—this book would not exist. They were willing and able to share not only their knowledge, but also their enthusiasm and support. My hat is off to each one of them.

Thank God for friends! The contributions and words of encouragment of my two dear friends and colleagues, Karin Mohtadi and Vivian Schlessinger, helped me on more than one occasion. My buddy Jacqueline Joseph and other members of the Portland Bag Ladies (Business Action Group) also offered moral support.

This is my first book, and Reva Basch, John Bryans, and Janet Spavlik of Information Today, and Patty Shannon of The Work Station helped make putting it together as stressless and enjoyable as possible. In fact, I'd even consider doing another Super Searchers book!

My husband, Greg, deserves a round of applause for listening to my endless talk about "the book" and giving me years of love and encouragement.

Introduction

When I told people I was putting together a book on researching mergers and acquisitions (M&A), I usually received a blank stare. But those of you who are familiar with researching business issues, or who see the need to be familiar with researching business issues, will agree that it is an area worth investigation. Every year is a record-breaking year in terms of the number of deals and the total value of those deals. According to Mergerstat, in 1990 there were 2,074 transactions valued over $1 million; in 1995 there were 3,510; and in 1999 there were 9,278! And it's hard, even for those with minimal interest in corporate restructuring, to ignore headlines like "AOL Acquires Time Warner—the Biggest Deal Ever."

As Bruce Wasserstein writes in the introduction to his bestseller, *Big Deal*, "Growth by merger has been a part of American economic history since the coming of the Industrial Revolution." Wasserstein goes on to say, "Still, good, bad, or indifferent, mergers and acquisitions are an essential vehicle for corporate change, and the pace of change is increasing." Researchers are no doubt affected by the continual growth in M&A activity.

RESEARCH ENVIRONMENT

Information and business professionals in investment banks, business valuation firms, business brokerages, universities, and independent consultancies need to find information relating to mergers and acquisitions—or M&A, as it is more commonly called. The majority of the interviews in this book are with information professionals who routinely are asked to find information for someone who is playing a principal role in an M&A transaction.

But I've also interviewed business professionals who are involved in M&A for other reasons, such as representing the seller of a business or using transaction data to help in the valuation of a privately held company. I'm glad I included these noninformation specialists, Rob Schlegel and Jack Sanders, because they provide a much needed context for M&A research. Just about every information specialist I interviewed asserted that it is extremely important to understand not only the data they are researching but also *why* they are researching the data.

Interviews with data providers, such as Rob Teitelman of *The Daily Deal* and Jim Mallea of Thomson Financial Securities Data (TFSD), gave a different viewpoint on M&A research. Both are involved in gathering, analyzing, and arranging the raw data in a useful format for searchers. As any Super Searcher will attest, it is one thing to know how to use the databases; it is another to understand the strengths and weaknesses of the data.

Investment Banks

I interviewed several information specialists for *Super Seachers on Mergers & Acquisitions* who work or have worked with the investment bankers who are integrally involved in structuring, advising, negotiating, valuing, and executing the deals. Investment bankers and analysts rely heavily on experts like Penny Cagan, Bruce Liebman, Ed Vazquez, and Sylvia James, to find transaction information such as the number of deals that have taken place in a certain industry, or what other investment banks have done, or to obtain financial ratios.

Penny, a Super Searcher with years of experience on Wall Street, relates, "Investment bankers ask for a lot of industry research, and they want it very quickly." Company information of all types is very important to the bankers. Their frequent questions such as "Who owns the stock?", "Can I get news about the company?", and "I need a list of their mergers" are what Bruce calls "meatball reference." [*Editor's note: "Meatball searching," a term coined by librarian Robert Jack, is a play on the M*A*S*H TV series' phrase, "meatball surgery."*] Investment bankers also ask information specialists to do competitive intelligence for their firms, as well as to join in their marketing efforts by prospecting for new clients.

Business Appraisers

Investment bankers aren't the only business professionals involved with buying and selling businesses. Business appraisers are extremely busy these days valuing privately held companies. In fact, the business valuation industry will continue to enjoy favorable demographic conditions as the number of privately held businesses sold or passed on to family members increases with the aging baby boomer generation. Business valuations, or appraisals, are done for a number of reasons such as gift and estate tax work, marital dissolution settlements, the sale of a business, or corporate planning. Business valuation involves placing a price or value on a stock that is not publicly traded. M&A transaction data, or market data in the business appraisal world, can provide guidance on what that value should be.

Business appraisers look at M&A transaction data in order to find financial ratios that will help them determine the valuation of their client's business. As appraiser Rob Schlegel said in his interview, "It's important to use transaction data because they provide solid evidence of market patterns and dynamics." However, above and beyond transaction data, information specialists and appraisers also research industry and economic information. Rob goes on to say that this information "is absolutely vital" in a business valuation because industry and economic forces have a large impact on how a company operates.

Law Firms

Law firms are also integrally involved in the M&A arena. Super Searcher and law librarian Luci Barry reports that law firms not only draft the agreements of an M&A transaction, but also advise all parties to the transaction of all the legal issues relating to the deal. Both Luci and her colleague Reed Nelson are asked by the firm's attorneys to help in the due diligence process. This involves searching public records, which means finding corporate filings, "dirt" on people, or court cases. Law librarians are also called upon to find exemplars, or examples of documents that are similar to the documents the attorneys are drafting.

I interviewed both Luci and Reed to see how two researchers within the same company approach research differently. Today, information specialists are confronted with myriad competing databases, and it is not surprising that each searcher develops his or her own favorite sources and strategies. Reed said a couple of times in his interview that "I tend to use the source I know best"— a sentiment that I'm sure is shared by many searchers.

Business Brokerages

"M&A" typically refers to businesses that sell for over $1 million. But what about all those small businesses in your community that change hands? Information on the sales of such businesses is needed by business brokers or business intermediaries. While Jack Sanders is not a researcher *per se*, I interviewed him for his in-depth knowledge of the transactions that occur between small businesses. Jack states that, in the U.S., the average small, mom-and-pop-type business lasts between five and eight years before the owner decides to sell it. In order to come up with a sale price, the company owner often engages a business broker to assist with the sale. Because those intermediaries frequently seek the prices of comparable deals, Jack developed the BIZCOMPS studies that report transaction data for smaller companies—data that are not contained in the databases used by investment banks.

Academia

Students often want to know about M&A for classroom-related research projects. Super Searcher Steven Bell is well-known for his knowledge of M&A data sources, particularly as they relate to the academic environment. Steven spent 10 years at Wharton's Lippincott Library assisting students and faculty with their M&A inquiries, such as what deals have taken place in a certain industry.

Those students who had exposure to M&A research under Steven's guidance no doubt received an early lesson in the amount and detail of transaction data available, as well as the pitfalls in that type of research. However, in order for academic libraries to provide the expensive M&A transaction databases to their students and faculty, it is imperative that academic librarians work closely with database providers.

Database Providers

Database providers are continually looking for ways to stand out in the competitive market in which they operate. Super Searcher Ed Vazquez, with his many years of experience working with large investment banks on Wall Street, was lured by a database provider to develop a new product that would assist those who were researching business issues, including M&A. Ed's previous experience gave him tremendous knowledge of the variety of databases that are used in assisting M&A bankers with their deals. He is using that knowledge in developing a database that combines the well-known fee-based online services with the untamed Internet.

I was happy to learn that database providers hire information specialists who have worked in the trenches, because Super Searchers like Ed know what type of market exists for a particular kind of information, why it exists, and how searchers prefer to retrieve the information.

Without a doubt, searchers need access to more and more information about deals that occur outside the U.S.—and, without a doubt, data providers are making efforts to expand the scope of their products to include these deals. Jim Mallea informs us that TFSD has opened offices around the globe, recognizing the fact that M&A is expanding internationally. (In fact, during the time I was conducting interviews for this book, TFSD acquired Securities Data Company (SDC), an authoritative source of M&A data. Rather than put words into my Super Searchers' mouths, I generally left references to SDC or Securities Data unchanged. The exception is the interview with Jim Mallea at TFSD. Readers will find a cross reference, in Appendix A, from Securities Data Company to Thomson Financial Securities Data.) Rob Teitelman mentions that *The Daily Deal* also has reporters in different regions where M&A is expanding, such as Europe and Asia. Mergerstat purchased CorpFin, a transaction that increases the database's scope of international deals, according to Super Searcher Mark Tygart.

Independent Consultants

Hundreds of business professionals do not have access to a specialized or in-house library. Most, if not all, of the databases that provide M&A transaction data are not available in local public libraries or the smaller university libraries. And in most cases, business professionals do not have the time or the expertise to do their own research. So, they call on independent consultants like Super Searcher Sylvia James to pull together buyers lists or assist in the essential due-diligence process. Independent research consultants often focus on a particular subject niche, as Sylvia has done with M&A and corporate finance. By doing so they are able to learn the information sources backwards and forwards and can do the research much better and more cost-effectively than the business professional could do on his or her own.

Sylvia has additional expertise in international M&A sources. A recent press release from Thomson Financial Securities Data noted, "The global M&A market is still red hot and record breaking." In an interview with the managing directors of the leading investment banks in *Mergers & Acquisitions*, the majority agree that globalization has had the most significant impact on the M&A market. Those of us who research in the U.S. are focused on U.S.-based sources. It is important to remember that different countries have different databases as well as different regulatory, economic, political, and cultural conditions, all of which have an effect on those databases.

RESEARCH REALITIES

Interviewing these thirteen Super Searchers provided many insights into the research process and environment. After the interviews, it was clear to me that researching M&A issues takes a certain type of person, not only because the research environment can be very demanding but also because the research requires a certain knowledge of M&A issues—things that would not have been taught in library school. Frequently, an interviewee remarked on a particular issue or trait that a previous interviewee had just mentioned. The answer I received just about every time I asked the question "What does it take to be a good M&A researcher?" was "*You have to be creative.*" I heard this answer so often that I felt as if I were talking with a group of artists!

Be Creative

Researching M&A issues is often not easy and straightforward. Lisa Doble Johnson says "Unfortunately you have to look in a lot of different places," and Mark Tygart adds that "M&A is a fragmented informational market because the data is not well-tracked. There is never enough information available." Just about every Super Searcher I interviewed stated something along these lines. Therefore, you have to be creative in the research project. It is easy to get used to one or two sources, and to think that, if you haven't found the information in those sources, it simply doesn't exist. But many Super Searchers stated that you can't be wed to the same data sources, that you continually have to think about all the possible places a particular bit of information might be.

Demanding Environment

Wall Street is a crazy, demanding environment. Those who work in investment banks and financial advisory firms know that long hours and quick turnaround times are the norm. Therefore, Penny Cagan advises having research strategies in place in advance, so you can find information quickly. Penny also states that, in such a crazy, high-pressure environment, it is particularly important to know how to manage your clients—knowing what type of research request is reasonable and telling them what you can and cannot do. "They expect us to be the experts when it comes to research, so why not tell them what is manageable?"

Investment bankers are under tremendous pressure, and that pressure trickles—or should I say *pours*—down to the library or information center. It is important to learn the style and culture of the organization and to know what your client wants. I had to chuckle when Bruce Liebman said, "...people not only want you to do the research, they want you to end up, almost, with the finished PowerPoint slide that they'll use in their presentation!"

What the Client Wants

The reference interview is important. Many of the Super Searchers related how important it is to know exactly what information the client really needs. The client may say one thing and mean another. Sometimes clients don't have a clear idea of what they want, and you need to educate them about the type of information that is out there. Constant communication is important. I loved what Reed Nelson said with regard to the reference interview: "Get the most complete information from your client that you possibly can—you know, garbage in, garbage out!"

One Super Searcher told me that if she didn't understand some of the information she found and she felt uncomfortable asking the client to explain the issue, she would ask a more approachable professional down the hall. The important thing is that you ask *somebody* to help you understand the topic at hand.

Less Is More

I heard several times that it is very important not to inundate the client with too much information. In most cases he or she doesn't have the time, energy, or need to read through reams of material. Penny Cagan reflected that it is much harder to give less information. This is particularly true for those of us who want to share with the client all the good stuff we've found. Penny cautions us to remember that "They just want to get up to speed quickly; they don't necessarily want to be an expert." Bruce Liebman concurs: "People don't want to print out a huge document; they just want the answer."

Learn That "Stuff"

"You *do* need to learn that stuff." That's what one Super Searcher told me. What "stuff," you ask? All those issues and concepts related to M&A that your clients ask for, such as what's in a proxy and why, or what are the different multiples. Without a doubt, practically everyone I interviewed stressed how important it is to know the basics of corporate finance as it relates to M&A—to know the jargon, the relevant Securities and Exchange Commission filings and what is contained in them, and the basic principles of accounting. "*Read*" was the mandate I heard more than once. Many of the Super Searchers began with very little, if any, background in business or finance. They taught themselves on the job by reading as much as possible, asking questions, and going above and beyond the call of duty in order to provide excellent research results.

Is it worth spending extra time reading business and finance magazines? You bet. Ed Vazquez found it imperative "to get into the heads of bankers" in order to understand *why* they need the information. Becoming an expert in M&A research takes time and energy, but Steven Bell feels the effort will be well-rewarded because not many people specialize in this area, and your clients will definitely appreciate your expertise.

Public versus Private

More often than not, one or both of the companies involved in an M&A venture is privately held. Since only publicly held companies are required to disclose the terms of the deal, the research can become fairly difficult. In fact, Steven Bell says that "One of the greatest challenges revolves around whether or not the company is public or private." Finding information on privately held companies requires researchers to be—yes—creative. Super Searchers might pick up the phone to talk to someone at the acquired company, with the faint hope that he or she will reveal more details about the deal. Searchers often find more information than what is reported in a database by checking an SEC filing. If the company was acquired by a publicly traded firm, and the transaction represents a certain amount of the acquirer's revenues, information about the transaction, including the target's financials, will be filed in an 8-K. But if a huge conglomerate takes over a very small company, chances are that the corporation will not have to report the details of the deal to the SEC, and the acquired company won't be required to say a word to anybody about the price it just received! More often than one wants to admit, a search is fruitless because both companies are privately held, and no useful information is available.

Inaccurate Information

Data contained in databases is not always right and is often incomplete. In fact, I heard several accounts where searchers encountered data that had either been entered incorrectly in the database, was missing, or was just plain wrong. How do you know if the data are good or not? In most cases, the person interpreting the data, usually the client, knows his or her material well enough to spot errors or inconsistencies. Jim Mallea mentioned that investment bankers, the Securities Data M&A Database's primary users, "monitor" the database and report data errors to the company. Human error does factor into the equation, so do not—I repeat, *do not*—hesitate to call the data provider if you suspect the data you found might be wrong.

Use the Phone

It is easy to fall into the routine of making databases your only research tool. But, as Bruce Liebman says, "Databases and such get you in the door, but the information is often incomplete. So, we have to pick up the phone..." Once again, this underscores the need to be creative in your approach to research. Several Super Searchers described the telephone as the most underutilized research tool.

The Internet

The Internet has definitely changed, and is still changing, the way we do research. For the most part, I received positive comments about the Internet as a resource for M&A research. In the past, the transaction databases were difficult and awkward to search. Now, because most of these databases are available on the Web with more intuitive interfaces, they are much easier to use. On the other hand, Bruce Liebman remarked that the Internet hasn't changed much in terms of our usage of the fee-based services: "If we didn't have the Internet, we would still have access to all of our databases."

Without a doubt the Internet has played a major role, not only in the quantity of information available but also in the type of information. Government documents, company directories, and trade association reports are just a few examples of M&A-related sources available on the Net. But the quantity of information available complicates the research picture; the Internet is one more place to search and provides so much additional information. I keep reflecting on what Penny Cagan said about the need to have a strategy in place in order to do quality research in a short amount of time.

The abundance of information on the Internet has also compelled companies such as Data Downlink to hire people like Ed Vazquez to develop products that unite the Net with their proprietary fee-based sources. Although *The Daily Deal* is a print source, its Web version provides an abundance of M&A data gathered from its reporters and a variety of data providers. It would be tough to find a more current source of M&A activity than *The Daily Deal's* Web site.

Love What You Do

This phrase applies to any job worth keeping, but I heard it from just about everyone I interviewed. M&A research can be difficult and challenging, but it can also be fun and rewarding. To be a Super Searcher, you really need to love those difficult, challenging—and fun—searches.

Mark Tygart

Middle Market Information Specialist

Mark Tygart is an Information Specialist at Emerge Corporation, a mergers and acquisitions advisory firm in Costa Mesa, California.

mtygart@emergecorp.com
www.emergecorp.com

Mark, tell me a little bit about your background.

When I was growing up, I never thought that I would be an information professional. I think I would have much preferred to be a knight, or an astronaut, or something else that children prefer, but I ended up graduating with a degree in history. I had done some substitute teaching but really wasn't all that into being a teacher. One of my best friends was working in an antique shop, and at some point a person who worked at a business brokerage came in to shop and complained about the problems they were having with their research. My friend promptly exclaimed that he had done similar research when he was at Berkeley, and why didn't they hire him on the spot? They ended up hiring him about a week later, and he recruited me to come to the firm, the Geneva Companies.

How did you end up at Emerge?

When I left the Geneva Companies, there were a lot of ex-Geneva-ite people around. I began to work as an information broker with some of them for a while. Then some of the people I had done research projects for at Geneva started a company called Emerge Corp. I was available when the company was starting, and they hired me because there was a fairly high trust factor since we had worked together in the past.

What realm of M&A research are you involved with? Do you focus on a certain aspect of the M&A world?

My research falls into a couple of categories. Emerge does a lot of work for valuation purposes, so the research is essentially transactional. That means that we need to find completed deals for which the relevant financial data for the purchased company is available. We also want to know if a control premium was paid, if there was liquidity discount given, what the multiples were, and the particular industry information for that industry. We do this research at a fairly initial stage, normally when a client engages us.

What are multiples, control premiums, and liquidity discounts?

Multiples are the financial numbers that are representative of a transaction and are used as a shorthand way of talking about what price was paid for a business. Multiples are usually a fancy way of saying how much your business is really making. The key metrics are EBITDA or EBIT. EBIT means earnings before interest and taxes, and EBITDA means earnings before interest, taxes, depreciation, and amortization. By looking at a transaction we might discover that a $20 million green widget manufacturer might be selling for five times its EBITDA. The "five times its EBITDA" is a multiple.

A control premium has to do with the amount paid for the control of a business, in other words, fifty-one percent or more of the company. Premiums are often paid because a controlling interest in a business is usually worth more than a minority interest. A control premium is a discount paid for a minority interest because minority interests do not share the same benefits as a controlling interest. Minority interests are also more difficult to sell.

Liquidity discounts are often applied for liquidity—how fast you can buy and sell the stock. A public stock is more liquid because you can call your broker and simply sell all of it. This makes a public stock more valuable.

Is all this information always available for any given deal?

No, no, it is not. In fact, M&A is a fragmented informational market because the data is not well-tracked. There is never enough information available, especially the hard financial numbers that people need to do their financial analysis.

Emerge's Web site states that it provides M&A advisory services to private, middle market companies. What exactly does "middle market" mean?

"Middle market" is a rough term. We tend to use it to describe firms that have roughly $10 million to $100 million in revenue. Middle market is sort of the Twilight Zone, if you will. It's everything that's not Wall Street, and not really brokerage or Main Street. It's everything that falls in between.

What size deals are considered "Wall Street" or "brokerage" or "Main Street?"

Wall Street deals sell for $100 million and over, whereas Main Street deals sell for under $1 million. Brokerages typically handle the transactions of companies that sell for $1 million or under.

Describe a typical client that engages your firm's services for valuation.

We define our clients in two groups. Our typical clients are the more traditional brick-and-mortar types of businesses. They tend to be job shops, particularly in aerospace, electronics, manufacturing, and capital equipment industries, or fairly high-level service industries such as computer integrators. We also have an Internet practice group; I would consider Internet businesses to be atypical clients by definition because the standard valuation metrics don't usually apply.

So, for instance, a company that makes sensors would come to Emerge and engage your services to value their company, so they can sell it?

Yes. Emerge performs a valuation exercise simply because we need to know what ballpark we're in. In other words, we need to know what other people are paying for these types of companies and what the issues are. Once we've done a valuation, we need to sit back and try to find out who would be a good buyer. In fact, a lot of my research is focused on finding a buyer. I look at deals and try to figure out who's buying and why.

How do you start? Describe your typical research project.

I'll describe a deal, actually. Typically, the financial professional will want a very broad overview of the industry in which the client participates. So, he'll say to me, "Mark, I have a semiconductor capital equipment client. Could you prepare some material for me to read so I can be up-to-date on what's happening in that market before I talk to him?" That's a very general, relatively simple, request for which I might pick up *U.S. Industry and Trade Outlook* [151, see Appendix A] or the Standard & Poor's *Industry Surveys* [142]. I may also do a quick and simple Mergerstat [101] or DoneDeals [46] search to try to find any recent transactions and deal multiples.

You just mentioned two sources, Mergerstat and DoneDeals. Can you describe these databases?

Let me back up and talk about the variety of information services that sell transaction data. Securities Data Company's (SDC) Worldwide M&A Database [163] tends to have the most data for the most expensive price. SDC also tends to provide data that centers on the higher end of the market, such as the large deals you might read about in *The Wall Street Journal.* Mergerstat is slightly more of a "hit" because it's cheaper and has more of the smaller, private deals.

Other sources we use a lot are DoneDeals and Pratt's Stats [121; now Business Valuation Resources], as well as BIZCOMPS [16] for extremely small deals. These databases, so far, don't cover the volume of deals that Securities Data or Mergerstat includes, but their pricing is more reasonable. I like using DoneDeals in particular because its one-time flat fee lets me play with it a little more. For instance, let's say I notice during a DoneDeals search that a number of French utilities have started buying American software companies, and I want to know what's going on with this trend. I discover that the French utility owns a publishing division, and I find out that a number of French publishers are very interested in buying American software companies, particularly ones that manufacture computer games. Because of the way DoneDeals is priced, I am able to do a lot more back-and-forth searching to learn more about trends like that.

The flexibility offered by a flat-fee subscription helps your research.

Yes, and that's very important. Being able to use a database without worrying about running up a huge bill allows me to be more creative in searching for patterns in merger activity.

Tracing trends back and forth is illuminating because many of our clients are convinced that their buyer will be their competitor. But after some database detective work, we sometimes find that the buyer will be the guy across the street who's not even necessarily in the same industry.

How does the Internet fit into your overall research approach?

I use the Internet all the time, as a delivery mechanism if nothing else. I think of projects in terms of levels, sort of like building a cathedral. I know when I've met Quasimodo in the belfry that I am involved in a very serious project. The Internet is like walking down the aisle to the altar; it's a good starting place for certain types of research.

The Internet is also a very good tool if you know how to look at data critically. For instance, if you get extremely good at reading corporate Web sites, you can tell a tremendous amount about the company. You can learn a lot about a company by reading its help-wanted advertisements. If you see, for instance, help-wanted ads for eighteen Cold Fusion programmers, that might clue you in to the type of work the company is focusing on. Another example: Web sites often provide biographies of their chief officers. I'm a big believer that a biography is probably the best single source if you want to be predictive about a person's behavior. Knowing an executive's alma mater or favorite philanthropic organization can sometimes be predictive of how he or she will respond to a deal suggestion.

Do you have any favorite sites?

Oh, certainly—I have about 400 favorites! Say I'm collecting names for a buyer search. Finding the prominent trade association in the industry is important because the association can be really useful for developing a list of buyers. There are directories on the Web that link you to trade associations, such as the American Society of Association Executives [8]. There are also books that list trade associations, such as the *Encyclopedia of Associations* [52]. Each industry chapter in the *U.S Industry &*

Trade Outlook and the Standard & Poor's *Industry Surveys* contains a bibliography that lists the major trade associations.

A word of caution, however. It is not always obvious which trade association serves an industry. For instance, I remember working on an optics case where I learned that companies in this particular subset of optics were actually classified in the ceramics industry. The most important trade association for the purposes of my research was one of the large ceramic associations. I never would have thought of that, starting with an optics case. You need to talk to your client and find what trade associations he or she belongs to.

Aside from pay-for-service databases like Mergerstat and DoneDeals, do you ever find deal multiples on the Internet?

You can, but with limitations. The International Mergers and Acquisitions Professionals Association (IMAP) [78] does a periodic survey, but you have to be a member to access the information. There are sometimes discussions in chat rooms such as those on NVST.com [111], but they're controversial; chat room data tend to be more "rule of thumb."

I would imagine that you'd have to wonder about the credibility of the information itself.

That's a good point. I do tend to trust the motives of organizations such as the Association for Corporate Growth [13] and IMAP. I think these organizations are trying very hard to compile good information, but it is a difficult task. Not only do they have to find all the people who have done the deals, but they also have to get the brokers to divulge the specifics of the deals. In many cases, the brokers are not willing to talk because their information is proprietary.

With M&A research, we're generally dealing with a private market where one is not legally required to divulge financial information when the business is sold. Because of that, we're constantly following the press around, trying to find people who are talking about deals, or trying to talk to people who are doing public deals, or deals where one party is public, or where there's some reason why they're actually divulging the financial information. But nothing requires anyone to divulge, so that makes it like detective work for us.

You mentioned NVST.com. Tell me a little more about it.

NVST.com is a very interesting site because it acts as an aggregator of M&A-related information. They've done a very good job of linking up various sources of material. The site lists businesses for sale. In fact, there is a variety of Internet sites where brokers list deals for sale. But you have to be careful because the market is very segmented by size. Most of the businesses listed on these sites sell for under $1 million. These deals are represented by business brokers, not by the intermediaries who typically represent the middle market deals.

Would you use NVST.com to just get an idea of what's for sale?

I don't, generally; I might if I get really desperate. I don't generally use listing sites *per se* as a source of competitive intelligence because they work on a classified ad model, at least in terms of how most people have used them so far. They usually provide a general description of a business in a geographical area, but I would still have to talk to the intermediary to get more information. So, there's a real limit to the amount of intelligence I can gather from the site itself.

Do you ever use the phone for research?

The phone is probably the single most underrated and most valuable resource in the life of any person who is trying to collect information. The diamonds in the rough that I've received over the years have almost invariably been over the phone. In talking to some industry professional, you can find out things you'll never read in the press. Off-the-record talks with people in certain companies can provide you with some consultant-level insight. Knowing how to use a phone is probably the real art in the information-seeking industry.

I am usually interested in merger dynamics, and I love talking to trade journalists or reporters when I can because they tend to have much more of the information I need. In my experience, trade journalists are extremely friendly and helpful.

Is the middle market community fairly talkative? Will it share information?

I often think of it as being like the CIA and the KGB during the Cold War. Everybody goes for a walk in the woods and sits down and talks about the deal that they're working on and the problems that they have with their bosses.

Mark, you were recently quoted in *Industry Week* [66] about the valuation of Asian companies. Do you do a lot of research for valuations of foreign companies?

We do. We look at foreign buyers, among other things, because some very active foreign buyers are buying American companies right now. The article in *Industry Week* was actually about American buyers buying Asian companies. We see it both ways. We tend to be more interested in foreign buyers buying American companies, but we try to keep an eye on both sides.

In the late 1980s, there was a tremendous wave of Asian companies buying American companies. But if you look at the statistics today, the British have been the largest buyers of American companies. There are huge numbers of European and Canadian buyers, too.

In terms of your research, do you use different sources to find out about foreign buyers?

There are different sources, depending on the country. For instance, Mergerstat recently bought CorpFin, a British company that compiles deal information. Because of this acquisition, Mergerstat will now contain more European deals. *Acquisitions Monthly* [3] was another source I used to use for European deals, but that publication was just purchased by Thomson Financial and is integrated with Securities Data's Worldwide M&A Database.

You have to be careful with foreign situations because each country is unique. I once spent probably the worst week of my life trying to find ownership of a particular Indonesian company. At that point, Indonesia was under a dictatorship, and companies weren't legally required to file much financial documentation, let alone list the owners of the business. The particular business I was researching was owned through shell companies and people whose titles did not actually correspond to their authority. It was a maze of mirrors.

It sounds like the type and amount of information you will find definitely depends on the country.

Very much so. The single biggest issue is transparency. A researcher needs to find out whether the country follows accepted accounting practices like we do here, and if companies are required to disclose financial figures. In South Korea, for instance, a person could essentially own large corporate entities anonymously. Competitive intelligence becomes very difficult if you have no idea who controls the company, or if you aren't sure that the person who supposedly controls the company actually does.

What do you like most about your job as an M&A researcher?

One thing I like about my job is that researching M&A topics is not easy. Because the research typically requires a lot of tracking and resourceful thinking, it allows information professionals to add a lot of value to the M&A team. If every market was extremely well-tracked, I think the job would be quite dull.

What do you do to stay current in the field? What do you read? Do you attend conferences? Do you subscribe to any mailing lists?

My research specialty is technology-related deals, so I read *Red Herring* [127] and *The Industry Standard* [65]. For professional associations, I prefer the Society of Competitive Intelligence Professionals (SCIP) [138]. I avoid most of the library science trade journals because I don't have the time to read everything. I try to get updates from the good vendor representatives and from friends in the industry. Information brokers are excellent sources of data, as market forces compel them to search for strategies that are both economical and effective.

What words of wisdom would you share with others who might want to do M&A research?

What makes a person successful—in many jobs, really—is personality. I have worked with people who were extremely intelligent and had a wonderful work ethic and were very gifted, but they didn't fundamentally enjoy the work. Often, these people view research as a steppingstone, particularly in financial service companies. They're hired as a researcher out of college, and they're looking to get on that deal team or to move up in some way. They start off doing research, but they don't enjoy it. That's the best advice I can give: If you don't enjoy the research, you are not going to be very good at it because it requires a lot of knowledge, patience, and persistence.

Super Searcher Power Tips

➤ We use DoneDeals and Pratt's Stats (now Business Valuation Resources), as well as BIZCOMPS for extremely small deals. These databases, so far, don't cover the volume of deals that Securities Data or Mergerstat includes, but their pricing is more reasonable.

➤ Being able to use a database without worrying about running up a huge bill allows me to be more creative in searching for patterns in merger activity.

➤ You can learn a lot about a company by reading its help-wanted advertisements.

➤ A biography is probably the best single source if you want to be predictive about a person's behavior. Knowing an executive's alma mater or favorite philanthropic organization can sometimes be predictive of how he or she will respond to a deal suggestion.

➤ Finding the prominent trade association in the industry is important because the association can be really useful for developing a list of buyers.

➤ The diamonds in the rough that I've received over the years have almost invariably been over the phone. ... Knowing how to use a phone is probably the real art in the information-seeking industry.

➤ You have to be careful with foreign situations because each country is unique.

Luci Barry

Law Librarian and Knowledge Manager

Luci Barry is the Manager of Library, Information and Knowledge Services (LINKs) at Gibson Dunn & Crutcher LLP in Los Angeles. Luci is a corporate information specialist who has moved into a knowledge management role with the firm.

lbarry@gdclaw.com
www.gdclaw.com

Luci, how did you get into legal research?

I have a degree in history from the University of California at Santa Barbara, with a specialty in Japanese history. I knew that I didn't want to be a teacher, and I heard about library school from several people. I looked into it and decided to apply to the University of California at Los Angeles. I was accepted, and I decided to focus my studies on database design.

My first law firm job was the result of answering a blind ad in the *Los Angeles Times*, which turned out to be for a law library position. The job was with Shea & Gould in Century City, California. I didn't have any legal background, nor had I taken the legal bibliography course in library school, but I was lucky enough to be teamed with a really good legal researcher at Shea named Deborah Farkas. I think my undergraduate studies of the feudalistic structure of early Japanese society served me well in understanding the typical large law firm structure!

While I was at UCLA, I had interned at the Boston Consulting Group and, while I was there, I developed some basic business research skills. The internship, combined with my strength in database design, really helped me with my new job because a lot of new online products were being developed and introduced at the time. CDB Infotek, which is now ChoicePoint [28, see Appendix A], had just come onto the market, and Lexis-Nexis [90] and Westlaw [160] were beginning to put up some news and public records files. I gravitated to doing more of the company and business research, while Deborah handled the legal research.

Shea & Gould closed their Los Angeles office a little over a year after I started. I had to decide whether to go back into some sort of database design work or stick with legal work. Gibson Dunn & Crutcher were looking for a corporate librarian and wanted somebody with a background in business research and database design.

A perfect match!

Yes. It was a brand-new position, and I was able to focus on my strengths, which were geared more toward business, company, and public records research than toward legal research. Gibson did not have CDB Infotek and some of the other public record databases available at that time, and they weren't using Standard & Poor's [141], or Investext [81], or the M&A Filings file on Dialog [94]. So, I was able to introduce the firm to some data resources that they had not used before. It was fun to introduce our user group to a whole new set of data. I got to experience this thrill again when the librarians at the firm were called upon to introduce the lawyers to the Internet. I've been at Gibson for just over ten years now.

Tell me a little about the firm and its involvement with M&A issues.

We're a large law firm—in the top twenty in terms of numbers of lawyers, according to the *National Law Journal's* [108] rankings—and we're one of the top five M&A law firms in terms of number of deals completed, according to Thomson Financial

Securities Data [148]. The firm is divided into five major practice areas: corporate, litigation, labor/employment, real estate, and tax/probate. We have offices in most major U.S. cities as well as several foreign capitals. I work with the Corporate Group, which covers both corporate finance and M&A. We have a broad base of clients covering the range from middle market to the high end of the financial spectrum.

Why does a law firm get involved in a merger or acquisition?

There are a number of reasons for attorneys to get involved in an M&A transaction. Both parties will hire their own attorneys to draft the agreements between the two. Companies also look to lawyers to do the legal due diligence. For instance, a company that wants to acquire another company will need to confirm that no one else has a lien on the company's assets. They will also need to check out the company's financial situation and whether there are any pending lawsuits or other issues regarding the company and its officers or directors that might affect the company's decision to proceed with the transaction. In the '80s and '90s, it became necessary to check for environmental problems as well.

Also, if the firm is representing the party being acquired, whether the deal is hostile or not, the company wants the law firm to check out the acquiring company to see if it's going to be a good fit. Lawyers are also involved in advising the company on the price and the terms of the deal.

How do you as the researcher get involved in the due-diligence process?

The attorney actually goes to the client's premises, talks directly with the managers and people at the site, and looks through the company's papers. The librarians usually get involved at the very beginning to find things that wouldn't necessarily be in the company's records—the environmental issues, information on the officers and the directors, bad press, industry information, and lawsuits.

Your research sounds like a pretty important part of the whole due-diligence process. How do you make sure that you've covered all your bases?

You really need to know your databases and their scope—and it's constantly changing. For example, public records searches are usually specific to a certain state and county. If you are unfamiliar with a state's coverage in a particular source, you might miss something. I remember when limited liability companies (LLCs) were first introduced as a new type of legal business entity in California. The California full-text databases weren't carrying LLCs in their public databases—just corporations and limited partnership entities. Since corporations, limited partnerships, and limited liability corporations are all "types" of entities, the natural assumption was to presume that they were covered in the database, and this was where the pitfall lay. Searchers looking for LLC records would probably have assumed that the entity did not exist, when in fact it did. If you didn't know that, and you looked for a company and it didn't show up in your search results, you'd say, "No, it doesn't exist. I've checked." When in reality, it might have existed; it just was not included in that database.

Where do you look for liens?

Information America [68] was the first, as I recall, to carry this type of information. Now it's easily obtainable in sources such as ChoicePoint, Lexis-Nexis, Westlaw, and Dun & Bradstreet [49]. Many of the Secretary of State offices now have their filings available on the Internet as well. Two Internet sites I recommend for accessing Secretary of State Filings directly are CT Advantage [39] and IncSpot [64]. However, because the sites need to be searched one state or jurisdiction at a time, professional researchers tend to use the third-party sources.

How do you keep up with all the databases and their differences?

For Secretary of State resources, our firm relies on our national corporate paralegal who specializes in the Secretary of State coverage. She and the library staff keep in touch with one another and fill each other in on any new developments. In addition, we keep our eyes and ears open for news from other researchers who might share their findings via electronic mailing lists such as Buslib-L [23]. And of course we learn the hard way—by making mistakes!

What do you like about Buslib-L?

Buslib-L is a listserv that focuses on business research. It is owned by Dan Lester at Boise State in Idaho and edited by Gary Klein from Willamette University in Oregon. Mailing lists such as Buslib-L should be an essential component of any librarian's tool box. They are a great place to learn about new products and new ideas, and are key resources for learning about problems with particular information sources based on others' comments and experiences.

What online sources would you consider to be paramount for a law library specializing in M&A research?

Lexis-Nexis, Westlaw, LIVEDGAR [91], ChoicePoint, AutoTrack [14], Securities Data (SDC) [148], Dow Jones Interactive [54], and Disclosure [45]. Aside from case law, Lexis-Nexis and Westlaw are both great for public records and the news. ChoicePoint and AutoTrack have fine products geared toward public records, including information on individuals. Dow Jones has a wealth of business-related resources. Disclosure, LIVEDGAR, and SDC have more Securities and Exchange Commission (SEC) and

M&A-specific resources. Washington Service Bureau's SECNet [158] site is also worth mentioning.

Would you describe some of the sites you use for EDGAR filings?

LIVEDGAR was one of the first pay-as-you-go EDGAR services to go up on the Internet. It has had a very good pricing structure since its inception. It provides full-text searching, field search-ing, and preformatted searching capabilities. Washington Service Bureau's SECNet was another of the early full-featured EDGAR Internet sites. They were the first to make Rich Text Format (RTF) versions of documents available, which was a sig-nificant step. Lawyers have to read a lot of documents, and the RTF versions are much cleaner and easier to read than the old ASCII versions. FreeEDGAR is a free resource that also provides the RTF option, as well as allowing users to select and download specific sections of a filing. That can come in very handy when all you want is three pages of a 600-page filing.

I consider 10-K Wizard [1], my current favorite, to be the best of the free sites for conducting research in SEC filings. They have an excellent full-text search engine, and the results take you directly to the point in your document where your search terms appear. You can limit by a number of factors, including Standard Industrial Classification (SIC) code or industry, and form type or form group. The only downside is that it is a cumbersome process to get into the entire filing since you need to click through several levels. You can avoid this problem by opening another window on your browser and logging onto the SEC's Web site, and using its EDGAR [51] site to pull up the full text of the desired item. For all of its limitations and lack of bells and whistles, sec.gov [152] is the fastest of the free sites when it comes to retrieving a specific filing.

How much do you use Securities Data?

SDC probably has more M&A-specific data than any other resource. Personally, I think they've gained their market preeminence by doing a little M&A work themselves—acquiring much of their competition over the years, so now they are one of the only sources for M&A and corporate finance data. As a result, they are often cited in sources such as *The Wall Street Journal* [157] and *American Lawyer* [5], and are considered to be a fairly reliable source. As with many information resources, there is a certain amount of incorrect or "dirty" data that you need to be aware of. Like Dun & Bradstreet, SDC obtains data from a variety of sources, and some of it is incorrect or unverifiable. Users should be aware of the limitations associated with sources that offer nonpublic, nonverifiable data items.

It *is* important to question the data you pull out of a database. How do you know if data are dirty or not?

It's always important to question a data provider, regardless of whether it's a commercial service or an online "freebie." All of the companies I've mentioned are reliable sources; however, not all of their data are reliable. This is a factor that all researchers must contend with, regardless of their area of expertise. We have learned through experience which types of information are likely to be suspect, and we take precautions and look for additional sources to confirm the results. We explain to our users the risks associated with relying on these data. We also monitor sources such as newsletters and mailing lists like Buslib-L to hear about others' experiences and to learn from them. In many cases, database data are incomplete or wrong, but that's the nature of the beast. Outside of SEC filings or Secretary of State filings, most company-related data are unverifiable.

How do you use Disclosure for M&A research?

I used to use Disclosure a lot, but there are many more products on the market now, and some of them do a better job in certain areas than Disclosure does. There are some areas where Disclosure is still the king, and they do have probably the most comprehensive group of SEC-related products. We mainly use it to pull copies of filings, both EDGAR and pre-EDGAR; for setting up alerts; and for its Section 16 product. Section 16 filings are Forms 3, 4, and 5, which selected individual shareholders are required to file with the SEC. I think it's important to know that Disclosure post-processes the information contained in its CD-ROM and directory products.

What do you mean by "post-process"?

The SEC filings are source documents that come directly from the company that files them. However, the data in the directory products like Disclosure's are re-entered and reformatted—or post-processed—because part of Disclosure's customer base wants normalized data. That way they can be sure they're comparing apples to apples when they make their financial comparisons between companies. It is a downside for us, however, because lawyers prefer to look at the original data. Again, you need to know your sources and pass the information on to your clients.

What books would you recommend for M&A research?

The bulk of M&A research is done online, not in books. Your most important resources in these situations are your database manuals. They tell you everything you need to know, including the help line phone number for all the questions you have that are not covered. Other than that, I consider the *Capital Changes Reporter* [27] an exceptional resource because it shows the background of the company and its stock. It documents everything that has happened: stock splits, name changes, a change in its state of incorporation, and so on. It is an excellent resource when you need to find out the true lineage and history of a company. Most sources only take you back one or two steps; *Capital Changes* takes you back to the beginning.

How does the Internet fit into your overall research approach?

The Internet is a fabulous tool for finding information on companies. In addition to the great directory resources such as Hoover's [62] and Wright Research Center [164], which is especially good for foreign company info, the Internet provides additional resources found nowhere else—the company's own Web pages. Even if the company is just starting up and hasn't filed anything with the Secretary of State, it will often have reserved itself a dot-com name, and this information is available from resources such as InterNIC [79]. If they've registered for a domain name, we can be pretty sure that they're serious and that we will eventually find more information about them.

Can you tell me about any other searches that you've done relating to M&A that were particularly challenging or rewarding, or just plain fun?

In the early '90s, the pre-EDGAR days, we were on the target side of a hostile takeover attempt. I was asked to find information about the acquirer, both as an individual and as a business entity. I needed to research the raiders' backgrounds and the circumstances surrounding each of the M&A transactions in which they had been involved. Most online public records resources only go back to the mid-'80s, and only a few news sources go back further. I combed every source I could think of, and I was able to paint a fairly comprehensive picture of the raiders' techniques and patterns in a relatively short period of time.

What do you do to stay current in the field? What do you read? Do you attend any conferences?

For the legal side, I keep in contact with my user group and ask them lots of questions about what they feel is important to them. I attend some of their meetings and other events, and I'm included in their in-house email communication. On the information side, I attend various conferences, including Intranets 2000 [80], Online World [115], SLA [139], and ASIS [6]. I read various newsletters and magazines such as *Searcher* [131], *The Information Freeway Report* [69], and *The Information Advisor* [67]. I also take advantage of networking opportunities, especially with colleagues in other areas of the field.

Tell me more about your role in reporting Gibson's M&A deals to Securities Data Company. What does that entail?

There are several companies, including SDC, that track the deals that law firms and investment banks work on and then rank their involvement in terms of the number of deals and/or the total value of the deals. I send several companies a list of the transactions that we've been involved with that have been publicly announced. The companies typically publish their rankings on a quarterly basis.

What are some of the research-related reasons to consult the rankings?

One aspect of legal research, which includes M&A research, involves searching for precedents. The rankings list gives you an idea of which firms do the most work in a particular area. You may want to limit your precedent research to documents drafted by the firms listed in the rankings.

What words of advice would you give to a person who is starting out in the field? What do you think it takes to make a good M&A researcher?

In talking with colleagues in other areas of librarianship and information science, I get the impression that the M&A research area is no different in terms of skills. A good reference interview goes a *long* way to performing effective research. Attention to detail is important, and using your own judgment regarding the validity of the sources you're consulting. I think the most important characteristic of all is creativity. Many times you will be asked to find information that is not readily available in any one source or item of data, and you will need to "create" that piece of data yourself, or at least get as close as possible.

What is your new role at Gibson?

My new role lies between the library and the marketing department, and centers on the tracking and reuse of internal data about our clients, our individual lawyers, and our transactions. The information I gather and reformulate is used for identifying precedents for research purposes, as well as identifying key experiences in specific areas for marketing purposes. I've gone back to my database design beginnings but with a much deeper understanding of my clients' needs, which is a great advantage.

Where do you see yourself next?

I expect I'll continue to pursue knowledge management and database design issues, especially in light of new technological changes. I enjoy the challenge of matching new technological innovations to age-old information science issues. I feel very fortunate to be an information scientist in the Internet era.

Super Searcher Power Tips

➤ The bulk of M&A research is done online. You really need to know your databases and their scope—and it's constantly changing.

➤ Many Secretary of State offices now have their filings available on the Internet as well, but because the sites need to be searched one state or jurisdiction at a time, professional researchers tend to use third-party sources.

➤ Sometimes your most important resources are your database manuals. They tell you everything you need to know, including the help line phone number for all the questions you have that are not covered.

➤ I consider 10-K Wizard, my current favorite, to be the best of the free sites for conducting research in SEC filings. They have an excellent full-text search engine, and the results take you directly to the point in your document where your search terms appear.

➤ A good reference interview goes a long way to performing effective research.

Lisa Doble Johnson

Business Valuation Researcher

Lisa Doble Johnson is Director of Research at Mercer Capital in Memphis, Tennessee.

Doble1@bizval.com
www.bizval.com

Lisa, I understand you have a law degree. How did you end up doing research on mergers and acquisitions?

When I graduated from law school, I decided I didn't want to practice law. But I realized that the parts of the law I liked were digging around for information, and research and writing. I got a job at Mercer Capital, a business valuation firm, to do research for those valuations, which includes researching mergers and acquisitions. And now I'm head of research at Mercer.

Tell me a little more about business valuation and why mergers and acquisitions pertains to that field.

One of the things that one might do in the course of performing a business valuation is to consider mergers or acquisitions transaction data; you could say market data. This is because what you're trying to do is put a price or a value on a stock that is not publicly traded. While there are several means of developing a value on that stock, market data can provide guidance on what that value should be.

There are three levels of value applicable to a business interest: a) a controlling interest; b) a marketable minority interest; or c) a nonmarketable minority interest. Acquisition data would provide the appraiser with multiples for a similar business when valuing a controlling interest in a business because, typically, transaction data represent the sale of an entire business. Multiples are ratios related to the price paid for an entity and to different balance sheet or income statement items, for instance, price/book, price/revenue, price/earnings per share, and so on.

What type of market data do you look for?

We look for whether it's an acquisition for an entire controlling interest versus a minority interest. The majority of our searches involve looking for transactions where the acquiring company purchases a majority interest or, at least, 51 percent of the target company. When one company acquires control of another company, more than likely they have paid more for that controlling interest of that company's stock than they would have paid for just a minority interest.

Knowing the price paid for control of the company allows us to approximate a control premium that we might use in our valuation if we value the company on a minority interest basis and want to move up to the controlling interest level of value. It also allows us to apply the pricing multiples derived from the terms of the deal in the valuation of our subject company. Some of these multiples might include price/earnings, price/book, price/EBITDA, and price/EBIT.

In addition to determining the price for which the target was purchased, we would like to find some of the target's financial information, such as historical balance sheet and income statement information, in order to derive some of the multiples I just mentioned.

Who are your clients, and why do they ask you to do this?

Anybody who needs a business appraisal or a valuation done is going to use this type of information. Business valuations are done for a number of reasons, such as gift and estate tax work or corporate planning. For example, if a business owner is selling the business and has received an offer for the company, he or she wants to know if that offer is reasonable. Then, we might look at other transactions in that industry to see what kind of prices were paid for similar companies.

How do you go about looking for these market data?

Unfortunately, you have to look in a lot of different places. Research for market data is challenging because a lot of acquisitions don't get reported. There's a lot of buying and selling that goes on among companies. But because there are no federal or state government mandates that require disclosure of the deals if the company is privately held, it is almost impossible to find more than a simple press release announcing the transaction. And these press releases typically do not include financial data on the deal. There are some places where you can find—or hopefully find—this stuff, but it requires some legwork.

What sources do you use?

The first good source I recommend is a publication called Mergerstat [101, see Appendix A], published by Houlihan Lokey Howard and Zukin, which comes in both print and electronic form. It comes out once a year, followed by a quarterly update. DoneDeals [46] is another excellent source which, as far as I know, is only available online. Mergerstat and DoneDeals both deal primarily with transactions where acquirer, target, or both are public companies. But they do include data for private companies, depending on the filing requirements.

Can you elaborate on the filing requirements and why that impacts the amount of information you can find on a deal?

Legally, publicly traded companies are required to disclose certain information in their filings to the SEC. Some examples of these filings include 10-Ks, 10-Qs, proxy statements, prospectuses, and 8-Ks. A public company is required to disclose information related to the sale of the company so that its shareholders are informed in their vote on the proposed transaction. We can access those same filings to determine the terms of the deal and underlying financial information. If a public company is purchasing another company, the acquirer is required to disclose information only if the deal is of a particular size in relation to the acquirer. When companies are required to fully disclose the terms of the deal, we can generally get good information. However, the majority of the deals that occur are never reported because there is no legal compulsion to do so. Therefore, detailed deal information can be limited.

When you use these sources, how do you construct your search?

We typically search by Standard Industrial Classification (SIC) code. For instance, grocery stores fall under the SIC code 5411. There is a newer system called the North American Industry Classification System (NAICS) that also categorizes business types, but only a few databases have started to convert to this classification system. Databases allow you to search for transactions where the acquirer or the acquiree categorizes its operations under a particular SIC code. This allows us to find transactions where the acquiree has a similar business to that which we are valuing. We can also search using particular points in time, particular locations, or keywords.

In what form do you give the results of the search to the analyst?

That depends on the database, but we usually print out the names of the buyer and seller, the SIC code of the target company, a business description, and any pricing multiples that might be available for that deal. Databases that focus on a particular industry type might contain more detail. For instance, a database of bank and thrift transactions will contain ratios such as price/deposits or price/loan portfolio. A database of cable television companies might contain information such as the acquiree's number of subscribers.

When you do these searches, what do you give your client? Do you put it in a spreadsheet or do any additional calculations?

That depends on what the particular client is looking for. At the outset, we might give the printout to the analyst. He or she looks at the initial search results because, in a lot of situations, the transactions will not be comparable to the company the analyst is valuing. If there is no comparability, we might need to do additional searches to widen the scope. Or it may just be that there weren't any transactions out there, and we may decide to do our valuation without acquisition data. If some of the transactions found in the initial search do provide some guidance in our work, we may do some further digging to determine more details and/or underlying financial information related to the deal.

Do you ever try to find any additional information beyond what is provided by the database? Do you ever call someone, or check a newspaper?

We have called people, such as the investor relations departments of some of the public companies, to try to interview them about a particular deal. The additional information we get from them is often sketchy because some people are not willing to tell you anything; they just say, "The terms were not disclosed and we don't want to talk about it." We've been most successful in getting additional information from telephone interviews when we've wanted to know additional details, such as why the company made the acquisitions and what they were looking at in terms of financial returns. Or we might ask them if they were looking at the target company because it was in a particular geographic area, or because they wanted to add a division that they didn't have before. Sometimes information related to why the deal took place can be really helpful in terms of analyzing its comparability to our particular valuation situation and in explaining why a particular price was paid for the target company.

Lisa, you reviewed a database called Pratt's Stats [121] for *Valuation Strategies*. Can you talk a bit about that database?

Pratt's Stats (now Business Valuation Resources) is actually a relatively new database, only two or three years old. It can be a lot more helpful for people new to the valuation business than databases like DoneDeals or Mergerstat, because it contains more information on the smaller, private company transactions. That is what a lot of appraisers are looking for. The database consists of more than 2,200 deals that have been provided to Mr. Pratt by a number of contributing firms—namely, people who have been involved in a particular deal and have disclosed financial information on each transaction. The database tracks deals with selling prices up to $100 million. It is quite helpful because these tend to be smaller transactions than those involving publicly traded companies. It captures private transactions, which can be hard to find.

What do you mean by smaller transactions?
A company that sells for $1 million,
for instance?

Sure, or a company that might have $2 million in revenue versus $1 billion. Pratt has really done a good job in providing a lot of details about the deals. According to Pratt's literature, the database reports seventy data items. It includes good financial information and a variety of multiples, including equity price/net sales, equity price/cash flow, equity price/EBIT, equity price/net income, deal price/net sales, deal price/EBITDA, deal price/EBIT, and deal price/discretionary earnings. It also includes helpful details about terms of the deal such as non-compete agreements, purchase price allocation, and additional explanatory notes.

Are there any industry-specific reference
materials that provide deal information?

Yes, there are several that I have used. One is compiled by Kagan and Associates [88]. Their database contains information on a variety of media and telecommunications deals. SNL Securities [137] maintains a number of specialized databases that provide transaction information in the banking, financial services, and insurance industries. We subscribe to their Bank and Thrift Merger and Acquisition Datasource.

Do you just call Kagan and Associates and
ask them to run the search for you?

We have a subscription to their database, which we access from their Web site. Upon accessing the information through the Internet, we can print out whatever is appropriate. Searchers can access the Kagan data by subscribing to the firm's Web site. Kagan doesn't offer contract-type research where you call them and they run the search for you, but anyone can do a search by subscribing on the Kagan Web site and paying per search. You pay only for the data you download, which is very helpful.

Do you ever use the EDGAR [51] database to find out about transactions?

The EDGAR database provides a lot of information on transactions. The database contains filings related to those acquisitions where disclosure has been mandated by law. The EDGAR database provides quick and timely access to the filings that contain terms of the deal, as well as underlying financial information. Unfortunately, the EDGAR database does not provide an easy means of searching for deals like you get with databases like Mergerstat and DoneDeals. One must search for companies in a particular SIC code, and then look for filings related to any acquisitions for the particular companies. It can be time consuming.

How else does the Internet fit into your overall research strategy?

The Internet is helpful in several different respects. First, many of these databases we've discussed can be accessed through the Internet. This eliminates the need to have dial-up access to several different databases installed on the computer. Second, the Internet has given us EDGAR and the ability to browse company filings and identify various transactions, which we did not have before. Finally, the Internet gives us access to a wide variety of newspapers and other media online, where we can look for press releases and other leads which might, after a little investigative work, reveal additional transactions.

What advice would you give someone who is looking for information on a merger or acquisition?

I would say that the search for information requires some persistence. There are some tools that provide valuable information. Unfortunately, the information you need is not all available in one place, so the searcher must consult a number of sources. I would also say that it helps to be creative. What we have discussed is by no means exhaustive. I am certain that there are other sources or means of identifying transactions that I have not used. Being creative in your searches can only yield more information.

Super Searcher Power Tips

➤ To do M&A research, you have to look in a lot of different places; it requires some legwork.

➤ We search by SIC code because very few databases have converted to the NAICS system.

➤ Databases that focus on a particular industry type might contain more detail. For instance, a database of bank and thrift transactions will contain ratios such as price/deposits or price/loan portfolio.

➤ If we don't find any comparable deals, we might need to do additional searches to widen the scope.

➤ We have called people, such as the investor relations departments of some public companies, to interview them about a particular deal.

➤ The Internet is especially helpful because it has given us EDGAR, and therefore the ability to browse company filings and identify various transactions, which we did not have before.

Sylvia James

Specialist in International M&A Research

Sylvia James is Principal of Sylvia James
Consultancy in Haywards Heath,
West Sussex, England.

da-james@11daymer.freeserve.co.uk

Sylvia, can you tell me a bit about yourself and your background?

I've got my own consultancy, which I started in 1988. It's not an information consultancy, it's more of a management consultancy. In Europe, where I mainly work, it's not really appropriate to have an information consultancy. People don't understand the terms "special librarianship" or "information" in the sense that they are understood in North America. What we really understand here is more of a research function. My consultancy, although it's heavily based on published information research, also does a lot of management consultancy work for both the users and suppliers of information. About forty percent of the work I do is concerned with mergers and acquisitions.

Before I started my own consultancy, I worked twenty years in London, mainly for all sorts of financial institutions and corporations. My last job with an institution was with Credit Suisse First Boston, where I was head of research. During that time I did an enormous amount of mergers and acquisitions research.

With respect to the M&A-related research you do now, what do your clients ask you to look for?

Most of the clients ask me to help them with the due diligence that is necessary for the preparation of a merger or acquisition. Most of the research I do focuses on looking into European companies for U.S. corporations, and into U.S. companies for European corporations.

What does due-diligence research entail?

When a company is buying another company, the top managers want to know as much as they possibly can about that company. They always do financial due diligence, which is performed by an accountant or financial specialist. But more often than not these days, they do what's called commercial due diligence, which means investigating as much of the company as possible from published sources. My role in the due-diligence process is to research the company and its market.

Say your client comes to you and says she is interested in buying XYZ company. How do you begin the due-diligence research?

We don't usually begin with the due-diligence research. If we're starting the project from scratch, the client asks me to do a company identification exercise. That involves looking at comparable deals because we might be able to identify a company that has bought similar companies in the past. If the client is working on a divestment, we might identify a company that is selling a company similar to the company they want to divest. But what we're generally trying to do is identify possible companies to buy.

How do you begin to identify those companies?

I've come to the conclusion that company identification is a great skill. It's a process that requires a lot of refining in order to come up with a list that meets your client's precise requirements. The client may be a small venture capitalist who's looking for a particular type of company for a management buy-in in his locality. He only wants to drive twenty miles—so that refines the search down enormously. Or the client might be somebody who is looking for a French company that will match his company's U.S. activities. So, it's really not a matter of using strictly electronic sources because you also have to spend quite a bit of time using old-fashioned print directories, and so on. Usually, what you're trying to produce is a list of maybe ten to twenty-five companies that can be further investigated.

It must put quite a bit of pressure on you to come up with those 10 to 25 companies because that's the list from which your client will operate.

Yes, but I don't feel it's pressure because it's a great detective exercise. And it is quite a kick for me to see the pleasure on their faces when I come up with a list of companies that, when they start to call them directly, are actually willing to go into negotiations.

That must be very rewarding.

If they're the right companies, yes. And that's the next step. They'll take the list of twenty-five or so companies and literally cold-call them to see whether they're for sale or willing to buy.

Let's suppose your client wants a list of ten companies in three European countries—say, France, Germany, and Britain. Are there a few sources you can name that are standard places to begin your research?

I certainly would never compile a list from just one source. That would be highly dangerous because I'm likely to miss companies. But one of the major sources I use time and time and time again is Kompass [89, see Appendix A]. Kompass is a very interesting publication. It's a franchise of a classification system that was developed after the war by a Swiss company and used to compile business-to-business directories. It has been adopted in many, many countries throughout the world, apart from the U.S., where it has always been a very lowly second cousin to the *Thomas Register of American Manufacturers* [147]. But Kompass is absolutely brilliant for doing company identification, and I will generally always use it.

To be honest, what I look for primarily is an industry source because it's generally the industry that drives the company identification list. If I'm looking for somebody that makes semi-sweet biscuits or some sort of widget for a machine tool, I need to find an industry source if at all possible. I use trade fair catalogs extensively for company identification. They're increasingly available on the Internet, which makes life a lot easier than trying to acquire them in print.

Do you have a very large library at your office, or do you use the local libraries?

I have a lot of key sources that lead me to other sources. Gale, for instance, is a long-established publisher of directories, such as the *Encyclopedia of Associations* [52]. But I do use libraries extensively in London. Again, it's a matter of what industry I'm looking at and what degree of refinement I want to get to—whether the twenty-five companies really have to be dead accurate or whether it's a quick-and-dirty search. Generally, I like to get it as accurate as possible, so I use whatever source might be appropriate. For example, a few weeks ago I was looking for a company in customer relationship management. Well, that industry was not exactly easily classified because it is a new service area that's a subset of data mining. It was extremely difficult to get a decent list for that project.

Do you use the phone to help you compile the lists?

Oh, yes, I use the phone for primary research, especially if I need to actually check whether the company does what it purports to do.

Would you call a trade association and ask them to suggest companies?

Trade associations are not my favorite sources because they exist to serve their members, and they're not terribly good at divulging information to nonmembers. But again, the Internet is making trade association data much more easily accessible; it is possible to find lists of association members that would never be divulged on the telephone.

What sources would you use if your client wanted you to prepare a list of U.S. companies?

I've used *Thomas Register of American Manufacturers* extensively. But in the U.S., you have a magnificent heritage, if you like, of manufacturing directories. Unfortunately, although they're literally into their hundredth edition, these directories are not fully accessible electronically. The electronic versions have been dumbed down so that you're only able to search for things in one or two ways.

Yes, I've noticed how so many sources that have migrated to the Internet have been dumbed down.

I'm afraid that really is the case for international sources, too. A lot of publishers seem to feel that they can just put the basic minimum into their electronic sources, with the result that everything that made a directory worthwhile is just not there anymore. Kompass is a case in point. Its print version is much more informative.

Do you ever use Dun & Bradstreet [49]?

Yes, I have to, really. All roads lead to Dun & Bradstreet. I have a problem with Dun & Bradstreet information in that it means something completely different in the U.S. than it does in the rest of the world. The credit connotations that it has in the U.S. don't apply in the rest of the world.

Let's move on to due diligence. Let's say your client has selected a company from that list you've prepared. What's next?

At the maximum, I've got two companies to investigate for a potential purchase or divestment. I've developed a methodology that covers something like forty-two different aspects of the information I know I need to research on these companies—on any company in the world, for that matter. I'm not necessarily going to get all forty-two pieces of information, but it enables me to do an analysis of published information that does not seem to be available. I call it a "gaps analysis" for my client. Some of the missing information can be filled in by primary research, but quite often it is requested from the client before the final negotiations of the company purchase. The information gathered in the due-diligence process is really important in an M&A deal, and unfortunately it's the things that you *can't* find out that they really need in the final meetings. Because the clients like to have as much as they possibly can, they like this methodology that I've developed over the years. It's broken down into four major source groups.

Will you share those four groups?

Yes, certainly. The first one is the legal and regulatory information available on the company. You know that companies in different parts of the world have different obligations, depending on their legal status, to disclose certain information for the privilege of limited liability. In such cases, a company's shareholders have limited liability for the debts of that company should it fail. It is easier to find information on companies in the U.K. because, if the company has limited liability, it has to file all sorts of data. Europe is also fairly strict with filing requirements for companies with limited liability, although there are pockets of noncompliance, like Germany. I also look to see if there's any litigation pending that might affect negotiations. It might be environmental litigation, or something to do with financial disclosure of information.

The second group is information concerned with funding or debts. I call this group "follow the money." This research tends to be for the larger public companies. By "public" I don't necessarily mean listed on a stock exchange because, in Europe, we have categories of companies that are public but not listed on exchanges. I look to find out if those larger companies have borrowed money at some stage. If they haven't borrowed money, I want to know that as well.

It is very important when a company is doing an M&A deal to know how much debt a company has. If the client is buying a cash mountain, he'd like to know that! But a lot of family businesses will not necessarily have disclosed the fact that they have a lot of cash. Or they might have plowed all their profits and cash back into the business. That's important to know, too, because they might have very state-of-the-art equipment or a brilliant staff, and you need to understand that. This kind of research is not so easy with small private companies, obviously. But there are countries, like the U.K. again, where you can actually track all the debt a private limited company has borrowed over the years because they file this information.

The third category relates to all the industrial and professional information about the company—what they do, what they make, what services they provide. I try to find as much information as I can, including researching their in-house newspaper as well as their technical processes, patents, and licenses. A lot of data are available in databases, but it has to be teased out.

The fourth category is all the information that's left over—information that's available to anybody and, essentially, coming from news sources. For instance, news relating to the company and any problems it might be having with a pressure group like Greenpeace or a union. This category also contains the never-to-be-forgotten books that may have been written about the company. I've been very lucky, occasionally, to find that a book was just published about the company, which set me up enormously and very quickly. It's so easy to do that these days with sources like Amazon.com [4].

So, that's how I structure the due-diligence research. This methodology not only provides me with a framework to present the information I found, but also with a way to indicate what information wasn't available.

You do a remarkable amount of research for each project, and I'm impressed with your methodology. For researchers who aren't familiar with European countries, where do you begin to find out what Spain's legal and regulatory structure is, for example?

The first important thing to understand is that Spain is in the European Union. The European Union has a whole system of regulation for companies because the European Union has decided that there has to be a level playing field across the countries of the EU. Therefore, Spain has to comply with all those regulations. So, before doing research on a Spanish company, you have to get yourself familiar with the company law directives and the European merger directive. It's very similar to understanding what all the various states in the U.S. require companies to file. It's just as difficult, or as easy, as doing that.

You have to have a good general knowledge about how the country you are researching fits, physically and strategically, into the economy. That is really important; you can't be a good company researcher, I'm afraid, without a good basic general knowledge of these issues. Some simple guides have been published about this—I've actually written one.

What's the name of your book? Is it available?

Yes. The guide is about official company registration. I call it *Official Company Filings in the European Union* [112].

In terms of the category you call "follow the money," how does one find out a company's financial situation?

You can now find information about the stock market and whether your company is listed on it quite easily from the Internet. A lot of stock market sites provide links to all the world stock exchanges. For example, I use StreetEye [145], and Stock Exchanges Worldwide Links [144] because it covers 102 exchanges. Once you've found a listed company, you're on your way because there's a lot more regulation than if it's a private company.

You must always remember that the private company sector is massive compared to the public company sector. So, more than likely, you're looking for a nonlisted company. The other problem is that a lot of countries still have quite a few strategic industries in the state sector—industries actually owned by the government. There's still quite a lot of privatization going on.

For those of us who always research U.S. companies, it's easy to forget about whether or not an industry is privatized.

It is a very important thing to be aware of. You need to ask yourself, "What's the likelihood that this company in this country is privatizing at the moment?" It's the sort of thing that you can read about in newspapers. I try to keep up-to-date generally, and in that way I have a feel for it. I can't honestly put my hand on my heart and tell you today that I know exactly what Vietnam's privatization program is, but I know, out of my general knowledge, that Vietnam is still not properly in the market economy. So, if I get a company that sounds like the Vietnam Oil and Gas Company, it's probably still in the state sector, and I therefore have to go into that mode of research, rather than trying to find it in Dun & Bradstreet.

Where do you turn for legal and regulatory information? I imagine it depends on the country.

Again, you've got to be aware of what percentages of coverage the various database hosts have. Lexis-Nexis [90] hasn't got the coverage of Asian sources that perhaps Asia Intelligence Wire [10] might have. Asia Intelligence Wire has very interesting directories of Asian company information.

You really need to know your sources.

It's not something that you just turn on like a tap. It's something that you have to increasingly become aware of and actually dedicate some time to learning. I'm not saying it's impossible to do; it really does creep into you.

What advice can you give about beginning a research project?

You should have an open mind. The trouble with a lot of information professionals' research is that it tends to be very bland; there's no imagination being used. It's easy to always use the same databases. You've really got to enjoy the process of doing the search. If you're just pulling stuff off the same database hosts that you use day in and day out, it's not very exciting.

How has the Internet changed your research? Are there times when you think the Internet is

just one more source to check, or are there times when you think, "Oh, I've got to go there first"?

It's just another methodology for me. Sometimes, it's extremely useful. Say I've got my company identification list and I find that I've got a wrong address or phone number for a company. Remember, we're going to call all these companies to check that they fit the identification criteria. So, I might want to do a quick check against up-to-date Internet sources. They might not be all that up-to-date, but they might be more up-to-date than a print directory. In a case like that, the Internet is absolutely ideal. I'd use a Yellow Pages directory or something of that ilk that I might find for the particular country using a search engine.

You mentioned a couple of sites for stock markets that link to all the different stock markets internationally. Are there any other meta-sites that you would recommend?

There are almost always some interesting meta-sites for each industry sector. Those often crop up in even the most cursory searches using one or two search engines. It takes skill to look for them and recognize them in a mass of unrelated sites. The relevancy indicators assigned by the search engine to a list of sites are not always a good guide; sometimes, these excellent sites crop up quite a long way down a search list.

For comparable deals, I've found some very interesting sites of business brokers who buy and sell companies. I have never been able to get at this information in the past. Brokers' sites have sprung up on the Internet because there is a great audience for the information they provide. These sites sometimes help me refine my lists because I can find some interesting companies on them. They don't give me much detail about the companies, but at least they provide me with some names on which to do research.

Are these business broker sites country-specific?

Not necessarily. There are quite a few international ones, such as the World M&A Network [162] and Mergers-R-Us. [100] There are also industry-specific sites. For example, there's one on mergers in oil and gas companies, called AP Tech Resources [9]. It is particularly helpful because it lists not only the sales of the companies but also industry-specific practices such as licenses and farm-out. It is very common in oil and gas industry deals to farm out, which refers to selling part or all of an exploration and production license.

Let's talk a bit more about identifying transactions. Do you use Thomson Financial Securities Data [148], or are there other European sources we should know about?

I was very close to *Acquisitions Monthly* [3], but unfortunately it's been dumbed down. *Acquisitions Monthly* was an extremely well-produced source, but the depth of data in the magazine has been very much diminished, and they've taken out a great proportion of the smaller deals that used to appear, so I don't use it much anymore. But there is good news with Mergerstat [101] because they've merged with a British company called CorpFin [35]. This will enrich Mergerstat's data quite dramatically.

Does CorpFin cover most European countries' acquisitions?

Yes. It's not as good as *Acquisitions Monthly* used to be, but it has a backfile to 1993. At the beginning, it had an emphasis on U.K. cross-border deals into Europe and Asia, which is not necessarily all the deals. But it's certainly going to provide more access to information on European deals.

Are there any other Internet sites that you use to identify deals?

I use M&A Daily [93]. It has a wonderful archive by company and date. It only has a year's backfile, and that is a problem because in M&A work I often do historical research. In those instances, I need to go back and find comparable deals during a specific time period.

One other mergers and acquisitions source that also is extremely promising is a magazine in the U.K. called *Financial News* [56]. Every week, they produce something called "Deals of the Week," which covers European deals valued over ten million pounds. It's beautifully produced, with a page every week that includes all the details—the bidder, acquirer, advisor, price, and financial advisor. It's really excellent. It's going to be presented in an Internet site called MergerMarket.com [97]. But you shouldn't ignore the fact that this is available in paper. *Financial News* does have an Internet site, but unfortunately you can't get this particular table on it. Very infuriating.

Tell me about your most challenging search, or one that might illustrate some of the challenges and pitfalls of M&A research.

I did a wonderful one last year; it's probably subject to a confidentiality agreement so I'm not going to tell you who it was. But I *can* tell you that it was a steel works service provider.

These are the companies that go in and clean up steel works after the steel has been manufactured. They clean out the blast furnace or whatever it's called—the place where the steel is actually melted from the ore. The company will take the slag from the steel works and convert it into briquettes that can be burned. They'll use a lot of heavy lifting equipment to get rid of the nasty bits. I actually went round the steel works to check all this out so I could understand exactly what this company did.

Did you have to wear a hard hat?

This is real due diligence! The challenge was to find other companies in Europe that did the same thing. Unfortunately, the industry in Europe was incredibly fragmented. This is what often happens when you're doing this type of work. You find that there may be a major country in the world with one dominant supplier. But when you try to find a similar company in some other area of the world, you discover that the industry is totally fragmented.

That is obviously why this company wanted to expand into that area. But of course they're not willing to build business organically. They want to see if they can buy the company that actually converts the slag into briquettes, or they want to buy the company that owns the heavy lifting equipment. When I was doing this particular project, the companies in Europe were split up into all these categories; there wasn't a single company that was strictly a steel works service provider. So, I researched the briquette converters, and then I went into the heavy machinery owners, which went into plant hire—those companies that hire out heavy equipment, mainly to the construction industry. Generating my list was quite complicated because I had to do it bit by bit.

Of course, my client understood this because he knew the nature of the business. Obviously, your client usually understands the business better than you do, but he expects you to be able to bring the discipline of research to pulling the information together, and he expects there to be gaps. I can't emphasize this enough; you're never going to do a perfect search.

I imagine you use the phone quite a bit on that type of research.

No, actually I didn't. It was literally a matter of collecting the raw data, sifting it, and putting it into some sort of order for the client. He didn't want to do it himself. Of course, I missed some companies. It was obvious that I was going to miss companies in this particular area because of the classification problem. It was so difficult to understand whether a particular plant hire company went into steel works, or was just involved in plant hire on building sites. But, by working with the client, I constantly refined the list.

It sounds like these projects take a lot of time. I would hope your clients understand that.

Well, yes and no. But don't forget that a deal does take a long time in its gestation. There might be competition or antitrust issues. The client may want to get all this information together because he/she is making a representation of buying this company before the antitrust authorities, and he/she will want to prove that the situation is not monopolistic. When the industry is fragmented, you're giving proof that he/she can take to the competition authority. Doing the research in an extremely structured way is worth a lot of money to him/her if it helps avoid a competition investigation.

Again, I always break the research down into small, manageable chunks. To me that generally means two days' work, maybe, spread over a week. I generally have to wait for bits of research to come in, or I'm waiting to do an analysis and I think of something else to do. Time to think is quite important. In that two days, I might spend a couple of hours thinking about how I am going to structure the research process.

You mentioned that one can never do a perfect search. Are there any other words of wisdom you'd like to share with M&A researchers?

The whole thing is an enormous challenge. You think to yourself, "I'm never going to understand this," but you have to start somewhere. So, you pick something that you think you *will* understand. Now, I did understand that they could convert the scrap that came out of the actual steel process into briquettes, which could be used for heating. So, I started with that, and I did the plant hire portion last. So, my words of wisdom are to start easy and go on to the difficult stuff later.

You must know a lot about a lot of things. I imagine you're very interesting at cocktail parties!

Well, I *have* been doing it for 31 years!

What do you like most about M&A research?

I think it's the thrill of the chase. It's the possibility of helping my client do the deal better. I know that if I do the research properly, the client will get a much better deal, and the integration process will be improved. The thing about mergers and acquisitions is that many of them don't work, and the ones that do work seem to me to be the ones where people have spent a bit of time doing commercial due diligence, understanding the company they are acquiring. I haven't got any proof, but I would say that those clients who have been fairly particular about how they perceived the company they were buying or selling have generally done a better deal.

Super Searcher Power Tips

➤ Identifying companies for a possible acquisition is a great skill. It's a process that requires a lot of refining in order to come up with a list that meets your client's precise requirements.

➤ I certainly would never compile a list from just one source. But Kompass is absolutely brilliant for doing company identification, and I will generally always use it.

➤ Primarily what I look for is an industry source because it's generally the industry that drives the company identification list.

➤ I use the phone for primary research, especially if I need to actually check whether the company does what it purports to do.

➤ I've developed a methodology that covers something like forty-two different aspects of the information I know I need to research on these companies—on any company in the world, for that matter.

➤ M&A research is an enormous challenge. You think to yourself, "I'm never going to understand this," but you have to start somewhere. So, you pick something that you think you will understand.

Penny Cagan

Wall Street Library Veteran

Penny Cagan is Manager of the Information Center at Operationalrisk.com. She has more than fifteen years of experience on Wall Street, including research positions with First Boston, PaineWebber, and Deutsche Bank.

penny.cagan@operationalrisk.com
www.operationalrisk.com

Penny, you have a lot of experience with the largest investment banks in the mergers and acquisitions arena. Can you tell me about the research you've done for those banks?

My first job on Wall Street was in the mid-'80s with First Boston, now Credit Suisse First Boston. Joseph Perella and Bruce Wasserstein were with the firm. They were two of the heaviest hitters in the M&A arena back then. That was my first taste of doing business research, and it was kind of wild back in the mid-'80s.

Why was it wild?

I joined a library at First Boston that I think was a little sleepy. And then all of a sudden, in the mid-'80s, everyone started doing deals, and companies started merging, and there was a lot of work to be done—a lot of deals, a lot of tight deadlines. Things got a little bit out of control there at the time.

Because of the number of deals that were going on?

Yes, and the amount of work that created. We used to tease each other because it was like working in an electronics factory. We'd work on three computers at one time. There were only two or three of us in the library doing research, and we'd put on our sneakers and run from computer to computer. It was kind of crazy. But there was a real energy and a real excitement back then. One of the first deals that I worked on as a researcher was the Capital Cities-ABC deal that First Boston advised. It was really fun to do the research and then see the big stories in the paper the next day.

What type of research would have you wearing tennis shoes and running around?

A lot of M&A research, even today, requires what I call the meat-and-potatoes research of an investment bank—searching SDC [148, see Appendix A], downloading equity analyst reports, and performing company news runs. We handled a lot of volume. An M&A banker would often give you a list of ten company names and ask you to research each one. But he'd kind of hide the name of the company he was *really* interested in because he didn't want you to know who the client was. I know it sounds ridiculous, but that's how they would conceal what they were working on. But then again, often it was legit—a lot of times they'd really want research on all ten of those companies.

What would you do with those lists, try to find as much news and ownership information as you could on each company?

Yes. Those were the days before end users had access to a lot of online sources. Obviously, with that kind of volume, and working on three computers at any given time, we weren't doing much analysis or value-added research. But we'd find everything for them—everything.

Where did you go after First Boston?

I went on to PaineWebber, where I was head of research. When I joined PaineWebber, they were not as heavy-hitting in the M&A arena as First Boston because they were a full-service firm. I thought I would be getting away from some of the craziness in investment banking, but a year later the same kind of volume caught up with PaineWebber. Once again I saw myself with a lot of companies to research. After 12 years at PaineWebber I finally left investment banking and worked in a consulting environment for a year, where I did derivatives research. After that I ended up at Deutsche Bank, and now I am working for a dotcom—Operationalrisk.com.

What was your position at Deutsche Bank?

I was head of research in Business Information Services. We did lots of M&A research, although the firm did have its own M&A library. We probably didn't get the volume of M&A research that the M&A library got, but we did quite a bit of investment banking research because the bank has a lot of crossover clients. For example, the bank will underwrite a company's stock, then, a year later, help them in a mergers or acquisitions transaction. I did a lot of work with consumer products investment banking, which involved looking at scanned data from Information Resources, or IRI [71]. This data allows bankers to analyze a company's division or product line and determine which areas are more profitable or need improvement.

Do your clients, the investment bankers, share some common perceptions about what's involved with M&A research?

They seem to think that you just have to push a button and the information shoots out. It's a stereotype, but it's true; they always want things two days ago! Sometimes the requests are totally unrealistic. For instance, they want you to get some document from a trade association and it's already after hours.

Investment bankers ask for a lot of industry research, and they want it very quickly. At PaineWebber, I always struggled between doing a really good job on the industry research versus getting it to them quickly. It's a real trade-off but, when you're dealing with M&A bankers, it's probably more important to get the information to them quickly. I noticed a trend that used to drive me crazy at PaineWebber. They would give you a research project with a one-hour deadline. I would be heartbroken because I knew I could do a better job if I had more time, but I would get them something within the hour. Then, two weeks later, they'd come back with a follow-up question and another one-hour deadline. It was frustrating. I felt that if the process could have been managed differently, we could have gotten them better information.

Why is industry research so important in the M&A environment?

It's very, very important for a number of reasons. The bankers need to know who their client's competitors are. They also want a sense of the industry as a whole, what the trends are, if it's a growth industry, if it's an industry that might go through future consolidation. They are often advising clients in industries they're not familiar with. They need to get up to speed very, very quickly on the industry so they don't walk into a meeting ignorant of what's going on.

What are some of your favorite sources of industry information?

I love TableBase [146], from Responsive Database Services. Another source I really, really like is OneSource [113]. It's gotten so much better because it has a lot of new industry publications. OneSource is great, especially if you're under time constraints, because it compiles information from a lot of vendors. For instance, say you're researching a supermarket. A single search in OneSource will pull up a menu of offerings, including articles on that particular company, articles on the supermarket industry, and a list of other supermarket companies. Then you can very quickly generate a really nice report that includes the competitor list and recent articles on the company and the competitors. It even includes write-ups from books like the *U.S. Industry and Trade Outlook* [151].

Often, especially if I'm operating under a very short time frame, I limit my searches to a couple of key trade publications. If it's an apparel company, I might just look at *Women's Wear Daily* and the *Daily News Record*. If it's a supermarket company, I'd check *Supermarket News*.

How would you identify the best industry publications?

At this point I know from experience, but there are reference books that list the key magazines. A good one is Gale's *Encyclopedia of Business Information Sources* [53]. I'd always check trade associations, too. I like to use the American Society of Association Executives [8] Web site because it links to the Web pages of a couple of thousand trade associations.

Do the bankers want a ton of information, or do you filter through and highlight things?

I'd filter through and highlight for almost everyone *but* M&A bankers because they never give you the time to do it. They just want to get up to speed quickly; they don't necessarily want to be an expert. That's why I would limit my searches to the major industry publications, and perhaps *The Wall Street Journal* [157], so that I don't get too much information.

Do you use mostly online sources for research, or do you also use print sources or the telephone?

When I started out in the early '80s, when the online industry was just starting, I'd use online sources maybe twenty percent of the time and books eighty percent of the time. Now it's the reverse—and I hardly ever use books. I fell in love with online databases back then. I *think* online. I've always liked going online and just playing a little, finding things that lead to other things. I love not having to deal with books.

How has the Internet changed your approach to research, especially when you have a tight time constraint?

The Internet has changed a lot, actually. For one thing, you can find information on the Internet that was very difficult to find before—like trade association information. Now I can often download an entire fact book containing major industry trends from an association's Web page. I'm no longer at the mercy of associations and governmental agencies; I don't have to call them because so many of their publications are on the Internet. That also means that I use more and more primary sources. Instead of relying on the references to a study found in an article, I can find the study itself on the agency's Web site.

I'm spending a lot less money online now that I have access to the Internet. For instance, I can get business wire stories about a company very quickly from the investor relations page of the Web site, and I don't even need to go to a service like Dow Jones where I'd have to pay for them.

Speaking of how the Internet's cut down on your online expenses, how does budget affect the overall research process, especially when a banker tells you he wants everything in an hour?

I've always thought about money, even when bankers tell me that cost is no object. Bankers have no idea how much money they could actually spend if you believed them when they said "cost is no object." And many research projects don't really require that you spend a lot of money. It wouldn't make sense to log onto Profound [123] and download a $2,000 market research report if someone just wanted trends in the supermarket industry.

Do you ever use SDC and Mergerstat [101] for M&A research?

I've used SDC's M&A database heavily, especially when we needed to know what acquisitions a particular company had made in a certain time frame. SDC is probably the best and fastest database for compiling that kind of list. Also, bankers are always looking at what's happening in an industry in terms of consolidation. With SDC, I could search by industry code and pull up a list of deals, or I could make reports that listed deal totals, transaction values, and total fees broken down by quarter.

Would you ever use the database to find out what the bank's competitors are doing?

All the time, especially when the bank is competing against another bank for a client. I would do a search by manager or advisor name and find out what deals they've worked on. If you are going up against a competitor, it's good to know what deals they have worked on and how the deals have fared afterwards. It also helps to know what ongoing relationships they might have. It is a vital piece of competitive intelligence.

Have you used any other M&A transaction databases?

I haven't. The problem is that SDC's competitors didn't have the same name recognition. The bankers want the authoritative source, especially when they're going to a client with rankings. It's standard procedure to do an SDC search by industry and rank the results by total deals, fees, or financial advisors. If the banker is on the list, it makes them look good. Because SDC is the authoritative source, they wouldn't go to a client with anything but SDC rankings. And, although SDC does miss some deals, it still has the broadest and most comprehensive coverage.

Can you recall one of your most challenging M&A searches, or one you'd like to brag about?

Here's one that happened to a member of my research team at Deutsche Bank, Rob Aiosa. The real estate banking division worked on the sale of the New York City building that appeared in the original Superman television series as the Daily Planet. For a presentation, the patron wanted a video from the television series that clearly showed the building. Rob spent the day watching Superman tapes at the Museum of Broadcasting before he found the perfect one for the banker!

What are some of the challenges or pitfalls of M&A research?

The challenge is to get quality information out to the client quickly, and knowing the right amount of information to give them. I think it's much harder to give less than to give more. It is also important and challenging to stay on top of the key industry sources and to be able to move from industry to industry quickly. One minute you need to be a quick expert on the apparel industry, the next hour on the power tool industry. You have to have the strategies in place if you need to gather information quickly.

What else would you want to tell someone entering the field of M&A research?

Knowing how to manage people, including your clients, is very important. You don't have to react to everything a first-year analyst asks for. That doesn't mean you have to be hostile; you just need to know how to handle it. You have to have enough self-confidence to say to somebody, "Well, this is really not very realistic."

A lot of people are afraid to say that. But that's what we're here for, to actually be the research expert, to tell them what makes the most sense. I'm surprised at how very senior, experienced librarians are afraid to negotiate with patrons, to tell them what makes sense and what doesn't, and to sit down with them and work it out. Somebody once told me that it took her ten years to be able to say to somebody, "Listen, young man, you don't really know what you're talking about." But you don't want to say it quite that way, of course!

Penny, tell me about your new position at Operationalrisk.com.

I've only been here two weeks and it has been a whirlwind of activity. I have worked in the risk field before, and I love the energy and intelligence. I am thrilled to be back and to be working with a small company; there are only forty of us. I was hired to manage a database of loss events. My team of researchers spends its days identifying events and analyzing the appropriate risk categories for the database. Of course, mergers and acquisitions involves huge operational risks because of the integration of systems, people, and processes, so my past experience is not for naught.

Can you say more about the huge operational risks involved in mergers and acquisitions?

Mergers and acquisitions involves myriad risks. The first one you have to consider is what we call "people risk." Mergers usually create unstable environments for a firm's intellectual capital. You have to ask yourself, if its most precious resource, its people, are packing it in and fleeing, what has really been acquired? This has been the case in several mergers I have lived through personally in the financial services industry.

Technology risk is often apparent; it is a big undertaking when two large firms merge their computer systems. Even something as basic as billing issues and how to meld together two different legacy charge-code schemes is a major headache. And there is often relationship risk—clients may feel uneasy about the merger and decide to move to a competitor. Employees who work for the acquired firm may feel bitter; there's a risk that malicious acts might be undertaken.

What type of M&A-related database are you putting together for Operationalrisk?

We look at five categories of risk: Relationship, People, External Events, Technology, and Physical Asset Risk. The problems inherent in a merger can straddle any of these categories. We currently have a database of over 2,500 risk events, including a nice sampling of merger-related ones. I am currently working on beefing up the records and adding analysis to the descriptions and a discussion of causative factors.

Is the database something that information professionals should know about? Is it available to the public?

Yes, of course! The value of our database is that it provides a succinct analysis of both controversial and not-so-well-known risk events. Our target audience is currently internal auditors and risk managers, but we have plans to market this to technology firms and corporations. The product would be useful in an investment banking M&A environment as a tool to make sure operational risks do not sidetrack a pending merger or acquisition.

I think it is great that you keep building on your M&A background. Where do you see yourself next?

I don't really know right now, but I do know that there is a lot of opportunity out there for information professionals—I have never experienced anything like this before!

Super Searcher Power Tips

➤ When you're dealing with M&A bankers, it's probably more important to get the information to them quickly rather than doing a really thorough job. The point is that they just want to get up to speed quickly; they don't necessarily want to be an expert.

➤ With industry research, if I'm under a very short time frame, I limit my searches to a couple of key trade publications.

➤ I *think* online. I've always liked going online and just playing a little, finding things that lead to other things.

➤ It is important and challenging to stay on top of the key industry sources and to be able to move from industry to industry quickly. You have to have the strategies in place if you need to gather information quickly.

➤ You need to have enough self-confidence to say to somebody, "Well, this search is really not very realistic."

Reed Nelson

Law Librarian

Reed Nelson is a Law Librarian at Gibson Dunn and Crutcher in Los Angeles. He specializes in M&A and corporate finance-related research.

rnelson@gdclaw.com
www.gdclaw.com

Reed, tell me a little bit about your background.

I have a master's degree in Library and Information Science from the University of California at Los Angeles. I've worked for law firms for the last eleven years. I'm currently a law librarian with Gibson Dunn & Crutcher, an international law firm and one of the oldest law firms in the West. The firm is very strong in corporate transactions, antitrust regulation, litigation, labor and employment, and business crimes and investigations.

What role do law firms play in mergers and acquisitions?

Attorneys are involved in mergers and acquisitions for different reasons. They are involved in negotiating the deal. Most, if not all, transactions need to go through a significant due-diligence process. Attorneys who are representing the acquiring company perform this due diligence to protect their client from any past wrongs that they may assume when they absorb the target company.

Attorneys are hired by either the target or acquirer's financial advisors, or by the target or acquiring company itself. In some instances, a company's major stockholder who wishes to dispute an issue or receive independent legal advice regarding the transaction will hire an attorney.

What is your role in the due-diligence process?

For the most part I perform public records searches. I research everything from Uniform Commercial Code (UCC) filings to litigation searches to popular news. Also, because board members of the target company are often given board membership in the newly formed company, we try to find background information above and beyond what has been disclosed between the parties.

What resources do you use for due-diligence research?

I use Lexis-Nexis [90, see Appendix A], Westlaw [160], and Dialog Corporation [44]. I also use CDB, which is now ChoicePoint [28], and AutoTrack [14]. ChoicePoint and AutoTrack allow the searcher to obtain data compiled from the major credit-reporting agencies. One of the first things I do is find out if the company is publicly traded. If it is, I look at the EDGAR [51] filings, like a 10-K, to see if the company is disclosing any pending litigation or dealing with a regulatory issue like a Superfund cleanup.

Dialog is an important resource for confirming intellectual property owned by or assigned to the subject company. ChoicePoint is useful for UCC searching, and is particularly strong in its coverage of California trial courts. I will still make the occasional phone call to a regulatory agency but not too often.

During your due-diligence searches, do you ever discover anything "juicy" about the company you are investigating?

There have been times when I've discovered a National Association of Securities Dealers (NASD) action, where the subject has been sanctioned in a securities fraud matter.

When you've finished your due-diligence research, do you write up a report of the results, or do you highlight pertinent sections of the documents for the attorneys?

It's very low tech. I highlight sections and write notes to make sure that they're looking at what I think they should be looking at. I usually end up giving the client a stack about three inches thick.

What other kinds of research requests do the attorneys give you?

I'm frequently asked to find exemplars of similar deals, which requires full-text searching in EDGAR. I recently did a difficult exemplar search where the company had issued warrants for common stock without a prior authorization. I had to find another instance where this had happened and the Securities and Exchange Commission (SEC) had okayed it. I did get lucky and found one.

What EDGAR system do you use for those searches?

Either LIVEDGAR [91], Lexis, Disclosure [45], or Global Access [61].

Why do you use the fee-based sources for EDGAR documents rather than the free Internet sources?

I'm very comfortable with Lexis and use its segment search capabilities to pinpoint relevant documents, such as an S-8 Registration Statement registering a specific type of plan, like an Omnibus Stock Plan. I also use segment searching when I need to target specific search criteria, such as finding a transaction involving a California corporation traded on Nasdaq that is the target company in a tender offer where the consideration is to be paid in cash only. I only use Lexis for searching, though; I always print EDGAR documents from a free source, such as 10-K Wizard [1].

What are some other examples of typical M&A-related research requests?

A typical but not very involved request is "Pull the most recent '34 Act filings for this company."

What are the '34 Act filings and why do they want them?

Under the 1934 Act, publicly traded companies are required to file with the SEC their securities traded on exchanges and the over-the-counter markets. Under the Act, companies are required to file periodic reports, such as the 10-K, 10-Q, and 8-K, in order to keep the public current and informed. These filings are a quick and easy way to confirm the financial health of a company.

Attorneys want to look at the exhibit list in the 10-K, for reasons usually related to due diligence, such as what material contracts the company has. The proxy is important because it lists the current directors, information regarding executive compensation, and a description of any stock plans for management or employees that the company may have.

Up until now we've been talking about researching publicly traded companies. How does the process change when the company is private?

When the company is private the research is much dicier. I pull the Dun & Bradstreet [49] record and any other public information I can find. I also do news and Web searches, but that is about it.

You said that you tend to use the sources that you are most comfortable with. Do you have a favorite with regard to M&A research? One that you just couldn't live without?

For finding examples of EDGAR filings, definitely Lexis and 10-K Wizard. I also use Securities Data's M&A Database [148] quite a bit to find out what fees have been paid to the financial advisors to the transaction, to compile lists of comparable transactions, and to obtain information regarding rights agreements.

What's a rights agreement?

A rights agreement is a document that confers certain rights upon security holders in the context of a takeover; they're usually referred to as poison pills. A poison pill is triggered automatically if a certain percentage of outstanding shares are acquired by an individual or a group.

Do you use any print resources for which there is really no good online substitute?

Journals such as *Corporate Counsel* [36] and *Corporate Governance Advisor* [37] because they monitor state legislatures, securities regulators, Congress, and other regulatory agencies with regard to developments concerning the activities of institutional investors, boards of directors, and shareholders.

How does the Internet fit into your overall research approach?

I often turn to the Internet after I have winnowed down what I need from Lexis. It's very rare that I go out and begin a due-diligence search on the Internet. I know that there are some free public records sites but, again, I have not felt prompted to use them since I know Lexis and can run searches that are efficient and cost effective.

I will say that, even with all the comprehensive databases available from the fee-based services, I may still need to do the same search on multiple services. I'll see something show up someplace that doesn't show up elsewhere. I can't afford to miss things. It drives me crazy.

Are all the public records you need available online?

By no means are all public records online. I often send couriers to obtain hard-copy court filings in contested corporate transactions, or to obtain hard-copy UCC filings when conducting due diligence.

Has there ever been a time when you just don't find anything in a due-diligence search?

Yes, if somebody's name is something like Bill Smith! But I try to do the best search I can by being creative, like making guesstimates about a person's age, or by linking public records through corroborating evidence.

Reed, how did you learn about researching M&A issues?

On the job. And Gibson Dunn is great for that because it is a very busy place and does a lot of M&A work. With all the work and the fast pace, I *had* to get competent. Once you're competent, work will come your way. It has definitely happened that way for me.

What would you recommend to someone starting off in a law firm who wants to learn more about M&A research?

I would recommend that they familiarize themselves with the '33 and '34 Acts, which contain the most common corporate filings made with the SEC. They don't need to read the whole act, but when somebody throws a term of art at you, like "Get me the latest '34 Act filings," then you know that you want the 10-K, any 8-Ks after the 10-K, a 10-Q, and the Proxy. Also, you can learn a lot by skimming through practice-oriented treatises. I would also stress that they should familiarize themselves with what is available in their local jurisdiction, basically just what gets filed with your Secretary of State and the Department of Corporations, and what is required within each filing.

What are some of the most challenging aspects of M&A research?

Getting the most complete information from your client that you possibly can—you know, garbage in, garbage out.

Do you get most of your information during the first reference interview?

No, it goes back and forth. A lot of times I pull stuff and take it to them, and I get "Well, this is good, but what I was really looking for was …." A lot of times they don't know what they're really looking for, and a lot of times you're trying to prove a negative, which is always difficult.

What does it take to be an expert M&A researcher?

I think it takes a natural interest in the subject, an eye for detail, and a good memory.

Super Searcher Power Tips

➤ Dialog is an important resource for confirming intellectual property owned by or assigned to the subject company.

➤ I often turn to the Internet after I have winnowed down what I need from Lexis. It's very rare that I go out and begin a due-diligence search on the Internet. There are some free public records sites, but I know I can run searches on Lexis that are efficient and cost effective.

➤ For difficult public records searches I try to be as creative as I can, like making guesstimates about a person's age.

➤ Researchers should familiarize themselves with the '33 and '34 Acts, which contain the most common corporate filings made with the SEC. When somebody throws a term of art at you, like "Get me the latest '34 Act filings," then you know that you want the 10-K, any 8-Ks after the 10-K, a 10-Q, and the Proxy.

➤ Get the most complete information from your client that you possibly can. A lot of times they don't know what they're really looking for, and a lot of times you're trying to prove a negative, which is always difficult.

Steven J. Bell

University Library Director

Steven J. Bell is Director of the Gutman Library at Philadelphia University. Prior to that, he spent ten years at the Lippincott Library of the Wharton School at the University of Pennsylvania, serving in a variety of positions including Assistant Director.

BellS@philau.edu
www.philau.edu/library

Steven, you've written quite a bit about researching mergers and acquisitions. How did you acquire that expertise?

I've been in the library profession for about twenty-three years, and all but about six of those years have been in business librarianship. I went to work at the Lippincott Library of the Wharton School at the University of Pennsylvania, where I learned a tremendous amount about business information research.

I got into the mergers and acquisitions end in an unusual way, by taking on a project that involved a bit of drudgery. When I started at Lippincott in 1986, I began exploring the annual reports collection because I was interested in company information, and in particular the kinds of information that can be gleaned from the reports and from Securities and Exchange Commission (SEC) filings. At the time, Disclosure [45, see Appendix A] had given the library a free, one-year subscription to a collection of annual reports and all of the M&A-related SEC filings, like the 14D-1s and the 8-Ks. The microfiche collection was a mess; you can imagine how many of those fiche there were. We were getting reams and reams of them, and we didn't know what to do with them or how we'd make them usable. Since I was the low person on the totem pole, I got the job of figuring all that out and submitting a report to the library director about what to do with them and whether or not we should subscribe to the collection long-term.

I had no idea what a lot of these documents were, so I got into the M&A literature and tried to understand what all the SEC filings were about. For example, what did it mean to be a five-percent owner, and what were the rules about tender offers—those kinds of details. I learned a lot from having to deal with that microfiche collection, and it allowed me to get more involved in M&A research.

Did having the Disclosure collection lead to more M&A research requests from the faculty and students?

Martin Sikora, the editor of *Mergers & Acquisitions* [98], was an adjunct faculty member at the Wharton School. Every other semester he taught a class on mergers and acquisitions. Another faculty member taught a higher-level M&A course that focused more on the finance issues rather than the nuts-and-bolts issues that Martin taught. So, we started to get more people coming to the library for certain kinds of information on deals and wanting to do database searches.

The library was a very early user of ADP, an early player in the M&A information field. ADP had a very useful database, although it was a little bit clunky. It was the library's first dedicated M&A database, and we used it quite a bit because more and more people required hard data that they were going to use for analysis. Searches for transaction data weren't possible using standard business literature databases like ABI Inform [2]. Also, ADP was willing to give us an academic discount, which was nice because, at the time, Securities Data Company (SDC) was not as willing to make its Worldwide M&A Database [163] available in an academic environment.

What were some of the typical M&A questions that faculty and students asked? You said they wanted hard-core data.

One of the most common questions was "What deals have taken place in a certain industry?" That must have been the number-one question. People wanted this information because they were analyzing an industry, or because they were trying to value a company within that industry. They needed to know what comparable companies had sold for. Consider it similar to buying a house. You want to know what other houses in the neighborhood sold for. It helps you in setting a property value or a sale price.

How would you begin the database search?

By defining the search criteria: What's the acquirer's Standard Industrial Classification (SIC) code? What's the size of the target? Is it an American company? Is it foreign? What output was the requestor expecting? Then we'd do the search to try to find other deals that matched the criteria.

Would you start with a database or with a book?

We had a number of books. A good example is the *Mergerstat Review* [102], which is an annual publication of deals. It's a good place to get background on how many deals were completed that year. We also used the journal *Mergers & Acquisitions* [98], because of its annual archive of all the deals that took place each year, the *Mergers & Acquisitions*, and the *Merger Yearbook* [96]. These were useful sources, but far weaker than the online M&A databases because the print sources listed only the most basic data items.

Do students or faculty have preconceived notions about researching M&A? Did they ever come in with a grandiose idea of what they were going to get?

Yes, on many occasions. They thought that every deal from all time was in a database somewhere, and that the database would be very easy to use. Then they would sit down and realize how difficult it was. We would have to take them through the search because these databases were not intuitive. You needed someone who knew all the codes and how to construct a search statement.

Does the library still provide this service?

Absolutely. About two years ago, SDC finally started giving the academic sector access to its information. Lippincott subscribes to SDC Platinum [128], which contains the Worldwide M&A Database, Global New Issues, Venture Financing, Corporate Restructurings, Corporate Governance, Municipal, and Healthcare Databases. Even if you don't have access to SDC, you can access the databases through Dialog Corporation [44]. Students now access SDC Platinum on the Web, and it is much easier than the old interfaces.

Tell me about the book you wrote with Michael Halperin, *Research Guide to Corporate Acquisitions, Mergers and Other Restructuring*.

The editor, who was at Greenwood Press at the time, saw the article I had written in *Special Libraries Association* [139] and wanted to know if I might want to expand on the topic and write a book. It's probably out-of-date because there have been so many changes in the M&A database marketplace. SDC bought ADP, for example.

Yes, but it's a good primer. It's helpful to know about the SEC filings you detail in the book,

because they contain data that the databases sometimes overlook. Did you ever teach students about all the different SEC filings you cover, like the '33 Act filings?

Not in a formal classroom environment. I'm sure my co-author Mike Halperin used that information when he taught his business research classes at the Drexel University College of Information Science and Technology. People don't necessarily want to know what all those filings are. They just want to get the information.

What would you do when you were working with a student and you just didn't find anything?

I guess one example of not finding "anything" would be finding only one or two deals when you thought there'd be more. In that case, we would restructure the search, typically by using a broader industry category. That's the nice thing about the online databases—you can easily change the parameters of the search you started out with. Before databases, that kind of research would have been very time-consuming, if not impossible.

Can you tell me about any challenges or pitfalls to M&A research?

One of the greatest challenges revolves around whether or not the company is public or private. It always comes back to that. When you get into areas where the majority of the companies are not publicly held, the amount of information available is certainly going to decline. You might find the deals, but the financial information isn't available.

That's another area where students got frustrated, because they didn't always expect that they were going to get a lot of private company deals. We would specifically try to steer students' focus toward public company deals. This is easy to do because the M&A databases allow you to specify that acquirers and targets are public.

Another challenge was when students would come in with something rather vague, like "I know I want to do something in a certain industry area." You'd do your initial screening and there'd be 5,000 hits. It was always a challenge to try to figure out what data the students wanted. Most of these database systems came with a manual that described all the available data, and students just weren't aware that so much information was available.

What did you like the most about researching M&A?

I think it was just the sheer volume of deals. The amount of action that was taking place in the M&A arena was amazing. It was a crazy field to try to keep up with, and at the same time it was something you could really sink your teeth into. At the Lippincott Library, I was the point person for M&A questions. There was a lot that I had to know, not only about M&A and all the SEC filings, but understanding the vocabulary and knowing the literature—the print sources, the databases, and how they work. The typical Dialog databases are structured very differently from M&A transaction databases. It is very challenging to become a specialist in this area. To really become an expert in M&A research will take a lot of time, but you will find yourself well-rewarded because it's an area where not many people specialize. People, both colleagues and patrons, will appreciate your expertise.

What would you consider the first step toward becoming an expert?

Fortunately, the current and past generations of experts, myself and others, have done a good job of identifying what is out there and what you need to know in terms of the sources to use. A lot of relevant knowledge can be gained by reading the available journal articles. I would also urge new business librarians to go out of their way to take on M&A research questions and to let people know you're ready for these questions. Do more reading to build your expertise; read and follow the M&A journals and other major business magazines that report deals. You can learn a lot by just picking up the jargon. Last of all, and the most fearful element, is to know the basic accounting principals and SEC filings.

Would you recommend articles published in journals like *EContent* [50], *Online* [114], and the SLA *Business and Finance Division Bulletin* [18]?

Those articles will really give you the flavor of what's required to do the research. If you understand the challenges, for example, of cross-border M&A research, you will know which databases to use when someone asks you to identify German companies that have acquired Japanese firms over a certain time period, for example.

Let's talk about your move from the Lippincott Library to your new position.

Working at the University of Pennsylvania and the Lippincott Library was a wonderful experience, particularly for learning and conducting M&A research. But, after eleven years, one likes a change of pace. I wanted to be the director of my own library, so I took a position at the Gutman Library at Philadelphia University. We have a fairly large contingent of business students, and a small MBA program. This job is a great starting point for me as a new library director because it isn't a large research library. The smaller scale is much more amenable to someone who's just beginning to direct a library. Still, the responsibility level is quite high. It was also a great opportunity because, in '97, this library was way behind the technology curve. When I first came here there wasn't a single public work-station where people could access the Internet. And I just said, "Well, we're going to be making big changes here."

And I'll bet you have!

Super Searcher Power Tips

➤ M&A-related information can be gleaned from SEC filings.

➤ I would begin a database search by defining the search criteria: What's the acquirer's Standard Industrial Classification code? What's the size of the target? Is it an American company? Is it foreign? Then we'd do the search to try to find other deals that matched the criteria.

➤ Print publications like the *Mergerstat Review*, the *Mergers & Acquisitions Yearbook*, and the *Merger Yearbook* are useful sources for an overall view of M&A activity.

➤ The nice thing about the online databases is that you can easily change the parameters of the search you started out with. Before databases, that kind of research would have been very time-consuming, if not impossible.

➤ Understanding the vocabulary and knowing the literature—the print sources, the databases, and how they work—is essential to being a good M&A researcher.

➤ Read and follow the M&A journals and other major business magazines that report deals. You can learn a lot by just picking up the jargon.

Rob Teitelman

M&A Newspaper Editor-in-Chief

Robert Teitelman is the Editor-in-Chief of *The Daily Deal*, a news magazine and Web site that provides a broad range of M&A information.

rteit@thedailydeal.com
www.thedailydeal.com

Rob, tell me about *The Daily Deal*.

The Daily Deal is a newspaper issued Monday through Friday, both in print and on our Web site, www.thedailydeal.com. It was started in September of '99, and its genesis came about because there was no daily information source or publication for M&A attorneys. The paper is owned by a private equity fund controlled by Wasserstein Perella, which is an investment bank. The fund also owns the controlling stake in American Lawyer Media, so it decided to explore the idea of the newspaper through that company.

We discovered fairly early in the development of *The Daily Deal* that the M&A attorney market was just too small, but that there was a much larger community of people involved in deal-making that didn't have a daily publication geared specifically for them. So, at that point, about January of '98, we started putting together *The Daily Deal*, which is designed to serve the entire M&A community—investment bankers, lawyers, accountants, consultants, public relations folks, regulators—all the people who gather around a deal. We've also expanded the audience to include corporate executives and entrepreneurs who do deals, and expanded the deal coverage to include venture capital, private equity, and financial buyers. At this point, our plans are to cover all financial transactions from angel investing and venture capital to large M&A, bankruptcy, and restructuring.

In a nutshell, we report on M&A developments, filings, and announcements, as well as financial structures, legal issues, pricing, and valuations. The reporters follow each deal through its duration, through the regulatory challenges, the proxy fights, and the shareholder meetings.

What is your role with *The Daily Deal?*

I'm the Editor-in-Chief. I was the first editorial employee; there were only two of us at the beginning. Before coming here, I was editor of a financial monthly called *Institutional Investor* for nine or ten years.

I noticed from the Web page that you have quite a staff now.

Yes, on the editorial side there are more than seventy people in the company. We were spun out of *American Lawyer* [5, see Appendix A] in early 2000, so the company as a whole has somewhere around 130 to 140 people. It's a little chaotic; we're growing fast.

I'd like to know a bit more about how your reporters gather information. Do they go out and find the deals to report on, or do the banks call you and say, "Hey I've got this great deal and I want you to report on it"?

We have about forty staff reporters and writers, and they do most of the digging around. We learn of deals from all kinds of sources; if a deal breaks during the day, we hear of it from wire sources. We also get information from tips and leads and leaks;

the reporters then follow it up. So, we find out what's going on in a variety of ways.

Reporters mostly have two kinds of beats. They either have industry beats—for instance, we have a telecom reporter, a utilities reporter, and a banking reporter—or they have deal segment beats. We have four people reporting on private equity, for instance, and five or six people reporting on venture capital.

Does the paper focus on deals involving publicly traded companies?

We report on any type of company as long as there is a financial transaction involved. Obviously, the easiest deals to report on involve public companies because the information is disclosed. But more and more we're delving into the private arena—venture capital, pre-initial public offerings (pre-IPOs)—where the information is scarce and difficult to find. You start with the big deals and work your way down. We're endeavoring to drop further down into the little market; we're doing a lot of research into the private equity market, which is, by its very nature, private.

Do the reporters make an effort to find financial details, such as the multiples?

Yes; if a deal breaks, the two things we would like the reporters to get right away—on the first or second day—are the names of the advisors, legal and financial, and whatever valuation information they can pick up. For instance, we run a fairly ambitious section, three or four pages a day, called Scoreboard, which is nothing but charts, graphs, and tables. Some of that data come from the 16 or 17 vendors that we have relationships with.

Can you name a few of those vendors?

Sure. The Loan Pricing Corp. [92], Portfolio Management Data [119], Computasoft Research [34], IPO.com [84], Data Downlink [43], IPO Financial [85], Venture Economics [154], Mergerstat [101],

NVST.com [111], SNL Securities [137], Stern Stewart & Co. [143], Bankruptcydata.com [15], Webmergers.com [159], PriceWaterhouseCoopers [122], and CommScan [32] come to mind.

The Daily Deal's Web site could save researchers a lot of time because you're compiling so much useful information from different sources. Will this information be available for free?

Most of the information on the site will probably remain free, but we *will* charge for some of it. We're continually expanding the paper; we're adding staff, we're adding content, we're adding pages—we're up to twenty-four pages a day now. The Web site was originally designed to be a mirror of the paper with a few rudimentary searching capabilities. But a whole group here is now devoted to building a totally new Web site. It will be a lot more data-intensive and a lot more customizable. We're designing it to have a lot of community, with chat rooms and discussion groups. It will also have some tools that people can use, which will make it much more interactive than the current site.

Is the information on the site archived?

Yes, all the stories are archived and the site has a search engine. We're also doing a couple of new things, such as providing mini-sites, if you will, containing all the information we can gather about fairly prominent deals. If somebody wants to know about the Time Warner-AOL deal, they can get the full range of data available on that deal from our site.

I noticed that the Web site has a section that contains rankings, such as the top ten deals in a given industry. Can you comment on those?

We get that data from CommScan. There are a number of important sources of M&A information—Securities Data, Mergerstat, and CommScan. We use CommScan and Mergerstat because they could supply more of what we wanted, and we did a better deal with them.

Since so many researchers are looking for deal multiples, have you thought of providing statistics on typical multiples by industry?

We do provide some of that information but, again, we don't calculate it ourselves—we have a vendor that provides it. We would publish more if we could get more. We don't have the skills or the staff to do it ourselves at this point, except on an episodic basis.

As searchers we are usually limited to the financial information provided by databases.

Yes, and often the deal universe is very small; you're talking about generating an industry multiple from three or four deals. For most public deals, which are the most transparent deals, the information is really good. As you go into areas that have become more and more opaque, like private company acquisitions, the information isn't as good. Trying to figure out what is going on in private equity and venture capital can be very difficult.

Would you suggest calling the deal intermediary to find more information about a deal?

If you're talking about a dealmaker at an investment bank, I think it might prove to be very hard to get ahold of them, unless you are a big client. Even if you did, I'm not sure they would talk to you. They're in the business of generating numbers that will argue their part of the deal. The data can be subjective. The investment bankers approach corporate executives and suggest deals, providing numbers to back up their case. It's the way the game works.

M&A is much more global now. Are your reporters trying to get information on international deals?

Yes, we have a bureau in Hong Kong, a bureau in London; we have fifteen or so stringers around the world. *The Daily Deal* is a startup, and we're trying to define, almost, this M&A community. What we are doing is going to get bigger—we'll see what happens!

Super Searcher Power Tips

➤ We learn of deals from all kinds of sources, such as wire services, tips, leads, and leaks. The reporters then follow up with more research.

➤ The easiest deals to report on involve public companies because the information is disclosed. We start with the big deals and work our way down.

➤ Deal advisors are in the business of generating numbers that will argue their part of the deal. The data can be subjective.

Jim Mallea

M&A Database Product Manager

Jim Mallea is the Regional Product Manager for Thomson Financial Securities Data's Worldwide M&A Database. Jim has six years of experience with M&A database management.

James.mallea@tfn.com
www.tfsd.com

Jim, tell me more about your work with Thomson Financial Securities Data (TFSD) [148, see Appendix A].

I am in charge of the U.S. M&A research team, although we have our hands in international research as well. We have been tracking the global M&A market since 1990, but we started doing regional research from several different offices about two years ago. We have researchers in offices in the U.K., Manila, Tokyo, and Melbourne, Australia. We also have a separate group that covers the Latin American market, although that research is currently done out of this office. Each office has somebody who heads up the daily research for that region of the world.

Tell me a little about the history of the Worldwide M&A database [163].

We would like to think that the database is the premier, global M&A product. There are some deals in the database as far back as the 1960s. As you move forward through time, the data become a lot more accurate—there's a lot more depth to it, and the quality of the information improves overall. The data starts to get good in the '80s and exceptional in the '90s. Even in the early '80s there weren't as many good sources of deal information as there are now. The Internet as we know it didn't exist, and there wasn't easy access to U.S. Securities and Exchange Commission [152] filings. So, up until the '90s, you won't find as great a volume of deals, and the amount of information that we report on each deal will not be as extensive.

Is the M&A database geared toward any one group of users in particular?

It is definitely geared toward the investment banking community, but all sorts of people use it—consultants, academics, lawyers, and so on. We have structured our product to allow individuals to access as much or as little information as they want to satisfy their individual needs.

Investment bankers use the database for several different purposes. One primary use is for comparable deal analysis. Say, for instance, that an investment banker is advising AT&T on a particular acquisition. Although he knows all the fundamentals of the target company that's being considered, he may want to find other deals where companies similar to AT&T have acquired companies similar to the company they're contemplating. He can go to the database to find similar transactions and say, "Hey, here's how X and Y and Z in 1999 structured their transactions. Here's how much they paid, here's what kind of multiples they paid, here's all the fundamentals on the company." When I refer to "company fundamentals," I am referring to the quantitative information that make up a company's financials, both balance sheet and income statement, as well as a company's stock price information and shares outstanding. It's helpful to know all the different aspects of the transactions, so that when bankers contemplate their own transactions, they have some basis for comparison.

The database is also used for general analysis. A banker in the U.K. might say, "I want to see how many deals there were in this particular industry in the first three quarters of 1998." The great thing about the database is that it's historical and there's so much information on any given transaction. We track about 1,200 distinct M&A data items, from the fees paid to the advisor to the target's stock price the day the deal was announced. Almost all the data items are searchable, so if you want to find every company that was acquired in 1999 for $12 billion or more, you can do that with one search. We gather tons and tons of information that our clients find extremely useful.

I imagine that you have to go to more than one source to get all the information to put in those 1,200 data fields. Can you tell me a bit about the process of gathering this information?

One of the best sources of information is the banks themselves, and we're very fortunate to have fantastic relationships with all the global investment banks. In fact, we have roundtable discussions with representatives from the investment banks as a way to make sure we are providing the data they need in the format they need. In this way, the banks definitely set the tone of the database.

With that in mind, I should mention that another important reason that investment bankers use the database is for the league tables—the rankings of the investment banks. Bankers use these rankings for marketing purposes. Before going to a high-tech client to pitch their services, the bankers will run a database search to find out where their bank falls in the ranking of banks involved in the technology sector. Then they can say to their potential client, "Hey, hire us, we were the top investment bank last year in technology deals."

How many banks report their deals to you?

Globally, a lot—several hundred. What's great about the fact that banks report their deals to us is that it's in their own best interest to get the data as accurate as possible because they're going to depend on that data for their own analysis.

Banks really help us make sure we have the correct information. Say there's a big Latin American deal that, for some reason, is pretty complicated and we can't get one really important piece of information that we need. We will call the bank and ask, "Can you get someone on your Latin American team who worked on this deal to help us out?" Sure enough, they'll get that person on the phone who will help us get that piece of information. Our users also monitor the database while doing their searches and report any discrepancies to us.

What other sources do you use to get deal data?

We use a lot of news sources. We're constantly combing through news sources looking for deal-specific information. Based on what we find, we gather and enter new transactions in the database, or update deals that already exist in the database. Say, for instance, a company announced a deal two months ago, but today they announce that they've changed the terms of the deal. Now we need to make sure we revise the data we have in our database.

We also rely heavily on regulatory documents, whether they're from the SEC or from the U.K. Regulatory News Service [150]. We look at takeover documents and other deal-specific documents from local exchanges. We've established relationships with the stock exchanges in all of the regional markets, so we can get documents from them, such as offering circulars that are the equivalent to proxies in the U.S.

I imagine that gathering deal information in other parts of the world becomes a little trickier because different cultures have different

attitudes regarding information and how much they're willing to share.

That's definitely true. In the U.S., there is fantastic disclosure. In addition to the SEC's filing requirements for publicly traded companies, businesses are very good about publishing press releases when they're going to do something like acquire another company. But you're right; because of local culture, companies in many Latin American and Asian countries don't want to disclose much information. Number one, they don't have to by law, and number two, it's not something they've done in the past. Those differences are something we definitely have to work through, but as time goes by, I think there will be more and more disclosure. Again, if you can establish good relationships with the banks and local stock exchanges, and do the research right there in the country, you will have more luck getting the data.

We used to do all of the international research out of the Newark office, but a couple of years ago we realized that in order to create a really great product, we needed to have people on the street who are familiar with the companies, the local takeover laws, and the local sources that we may not even be aware of in New York and New Jersey. Fortunately, we have done very well in training the staff internationally and getting everybody on board going in the same direction. All the various research offices work very closely with each other to maintain consistency and develop the database together.

How much tweaking of the data is involved before they're entered in the database? Say, for any given transaction, you have a regulatory document or a press release describing the deal. Do you just enter the information in the database, or do you question it or do any calculations?

I wouldn't use the word "tweaking," particularly, but M&A *is* subjective. You have to make decisions. You can't just look at a document and circle these twelve data points and stick them in the holes. We have very specific ways of analyzing the data so that it is consistent. When our clients want to look at all the apples in the database, they have to be sure they've found apples, and when they're looking at oranges, they have to know that every orange in the orange box is in fact an orange.

I'm curious about the information in the text fields, such as the business description and the deal synopsis because searching these fields with keywords can really help refine a search. Is there a company policy on how much information to include in those fields?

Yes, absolutely. While we track deal-specific financial information, we also track information on the companies themselves. We want to provide as detailed a description of each company as possible. Of course, it all depends on how much information we can find, but if a company has several lines of business, we want to mention each one in the text field. We want to make sure that you can find the deals. Otherwise, if you know a deal exists and you can't find it, you're going to start questioning the quality of the data: How could they have missed that deal? So it's very important for us, when we do the company research, to get as much information as possible. Describing a company can get pretty subjective; often we'll read an article and realize that the reporter may not have depicted the company very well. So our analysts really have to be able to read between the lines. The analysts are encouraged to call the company's investor relations department, or the person who wrote the article, to get more accurate information. In most cases the person on the other end of the phone will be very helpful.

I know that the database includes additional industry codes relating to technology. Will you continue to expand those codes, and are there any other areas for which you will be developing new codes?

We've provided detailed industry codes for the technology and Internet sectors, and we're constantly looking to expand our indexing coverage of companies within those two industries. If someone says they run an Internet company, what does that mean? Are they in e-commerce or are they an Internet service provider? Those industry codes are an area that we're constantly trying to improve, so that our clients can drill down and get the exact transactions they want.

Can the database be searched by NAICS Codes?

Not at the moment. But we will eventually add the NAICS codes.

What trends do you see happening in the M&A arena that might affect your data collection or the database itself?

The main shift I see right now is that the U.S. is no longer the clear leader in M&A activity. The European and Asian markets, for example, have seen dramatic increases in overall activity. What's interesting is we're seeing types of deals that we never used to see in Europe, like hostile transactions. In Europe, transactions used to be very gentlemanly; a handshake was an agreement. Now, all the various ways of structuring a deal that are common in the U.S. are starting to become more popular in Europe.

Is the financial data for non-U.S. deals reported in U.S. dollars?

This is entirely up to the client. We report every deal in its host currency. If a deal takes place in the U.K., we report it in pounds sterling; if it happens in Tokyo, we report it in yen. But the client then has the option of viewing the data in either the host currency, U.S. dollars, sterling, or Euros. The system will convert all financial and valuation items to any of these currencies.

Are you finding that there's enough data on the European deals—or any international deal—to calculate a multiple?

That's a good question. There are definitely limitations. We're always trying to get as much information as possible, but a lot of times, it's hard to get financial information on private companies. That's why it's very important that if we find an article that mentions a small Italian company's sales—even if it's the only data item from that company's balance sheet—it gets in the database.

How do users know where you got your data?

For each transaction, we have a field that lists the sources we've used.

Jim, do you have any advice for researchers who use your database on how to do a good search?

It's always important to manage people's expectation of what they're going to find. For example, as I mentioned earlier, we track the fees that the advisors have been paid on a given takeover or merger. The only country in the world that discloses that information is the U.S. A searcher may want to do a similar search for a U.K. takeover, but the data is not going to be there because the U.K. doesn't require companies to disclose how much they've paid their investment banks.

Then I couldn't ask the database to rank the top investment banks in Europe by the total value of their fees.

No, because the data simply do not exist. It has become the industry accepted rule to use the dollar value of the transaction as a proxy for advisory fees. It is assumed that if you are ranked number one or two based upon dollar volume, then you are also the firm that is making the most in fees. There is no set percentage that you can apply to a deal to determine the fee paid to each bank. The fee would also change based upon the type of transaction, hostile or friendly, and the overall size of the deal. Some firms will used the limited information we have on U.S. public fees and apply their own calculation to the international market.

Is there a way for searchers to learn of these limitations?

We provide definitions for every data item in the database. We also have a client support staff available 24/7 to answer specific questions about information in our product. Most of our core users have been customers for years, so they know the general accounting rules for the major countries and what each firm has to report.

Unless you know the ins and outs of a database—any database—you're not going to do a very good search. One of the good things about the Worldwide M&A Database is the fact that there are so many data points. But it's tough because you really need to know what they mean.

Having an extremely flexible, powerful database is a double-edged sword. If you're not a core user and you don't use it everyday, searching it can be confusing. That's why we run training sessions in different cities throughout the world, and have a twenty-four-hour support line for search assistance.

It's very important to let searchers know that they can call the client support line to help with their searches. I know I've done my share of phoning!

Absolutely. A lot of data items are very similar. Sometimes one will get you a more accurate answer than another. There may be a more effective way to structure that search to get the results you want. I would encourage anyone who uses the database to put our client support guys to work to help them out.

Super Searcher Power Tips

➤ One of the best sources of M&A information is the investment banks themselves.

➤ We use a lot of news sources. We're constantly combing through news sources looking for deal-specific information. We also rely heavily on regulatory documents.

➤ If you can establish good relationships with the banks and local stock exchanges, and do the research right there in that country, you will have more luck getting the data.

➤ Our analysts are encouraged to call the company's investor relations department, or the person who wrote the article, to get more accurate information.

Jack Sanders
Business Intermediary

Jack Sanders is a Senior Associate with Spectrum Business Resources. He also compiles the BIZCOMPS studies, which provide in-depth financial information on the sales of small businesses.

jsanders@bizcomps.com
www.bizcomps.com
www.spectrumbusiness.com

Jack, how and why did you become a business intermediary?

Do you want the long story or the short story?

The short one!

Okay, I had spent almost twenty years running a large engineering and construction business. At one point, a friend of mine who worked for a business and commercial brokerage called Page Olson thought that I would be pretty good at brokering businesses. He was very happy with the company and he suggested I talk to them. I did, and after speaking with the principals, I decided I'd give it a try. The construction industry had gone through a lot of turmoil in the early 1980s, so I thought the timing was right to make the change. Along the way, I had picked up bachelor's and master's degrees in business administration.

While I was in the construction business, we had a parent company and five subsidiaries. I handled all of the issues involved with running a business, including bank and surety matters. Initially, I thought being a business broker was going to be pretty similar to running a construction company, and I was quite surprised that it wasn't. Business brokering has much more to do with sales.

I remained at Page Olson for fifteen years, and it was an enjoyable relationship. During that time I learned how to do business appraisals. I became certified and involved with the International Business Brokers Association [77, see Appendix A] (IBBA), the Institute of Business Appraisers [75] (IBA), and the American Society of Appraisers [7]. However, toward the end of that fifteen years, I realized that Page Olson wasn't very progressive and, in fact, had changed hardly an iota from the date that I came on board. By that time, I had become friends with John Bates, who was the owner of Spectrum Business Resources [140], and he persuaded me to join them in 1998.

Tell me about the work you do with Spectrum Business Resources.

The change to Spectrum has been good because I'm focusing more on mergers and acquisitions, which has been my specialty for the last five years or so. In fact, since I've been with the company, they've actually dropped their business brokerage operation and are now totally focused in the mergers and acquisitions arena.

What's the difference between a business brokerage and an M&A practice?

Although they appear to be pretty closely related, there really is quite a difference. Most business brokerage clients, or the types of businesses they sell, are Main Street-type businesses, that is, small businesses with a sales volume of less than $1 million. The average sales price is probably around $100,000 to $200,000. On the other hand, the businesses that an M&A practice would deal with start at about $1 million, and most have sales of $10 million on up. I imagine that, if everybody had their druthers, they'd really rather work on businesses that have sales of at least $5 million.

Because they make more money?

They make more money, but it's also a different type of business. One of the biggest differences is that smaller businesses are typically owner-operated and are very owner-intensive. If something happens to the owner, the business definitely will suffer. On the other hand, larger businesses tend to be more professionally run and operated, with more layers of management, so they are not quite as subject to the problem of a single dominant person in the company. Although larger companies do have someone who is a driving force behind the whole operation, the company would suffer a lesser impact overall should that person leave.

Is there a difference between a business intermediary and a business broker?

It's more a term of art. The business broker, because of the connotation attached to the word "broker" as in "stockbroker," probably likes the idea of being an intermediary. It conveys the idea that an intermediary is somebody who would handle larger transactions as well.

You said that you are dealing more with the larger M&A transactions now.

Yes, only with M&A. It is difficult to specialize in both small and large businesses when, at one moment, you are talking to the owner or buyer of a dry cleaner or a deli or other small business, and then you have to turn right around and talk intelligently to the owner of a large manufacturing company. It's a different mindset and a different language. You pretty much need to bite the bullet and focus on either the smaller businesses or the larger businesses, but not both.

Who hires you? The business owner, an attorney, or a bank?

We're generally hired by the owner of the business. However, we're finding that more businesses now have a financial advisor interacting for them. Not necessarily an attorney; it could be a financial planner, or somebody who specializes in corporate financial planning, who will interview several different intermediaries and go through the whole process on the owner's behalf.

Do you report your deals to databases like Pratt's Stats [121]?

Yes I do, as well as to the IBA and, of course, BIZCOMPS [16].

How and why did you start the BIZCOMPS studies?

About ten years ago, a business appraiser named Brian Brinig had an office in the same building as my office in San Diego. Brian headed San Diego's largest business valuation practice, and he kept picking my brain for businesses that I'd sold, and asking me what the going price was for a liquor store, a dry cleaner, or whatever it happened to be. I'd search through my files and give him the data I found. I eventually realized that there probably was a real need, and maybe a market, for that kind of data. So, I started accumulating it and putting it into a small study I later called BIZCOMPS. The first study, back in 1979, had fewer than a hundred transactions. From there, it's built up to more than 4,400 transactions. Most business valuation professionals, brokers and intermediaries, and a number of business owners and buyers purchase the study. It is also available through NVST.com [111] and Pratt's Stats (now Business Valuation Resources) online.

How do you go about getting the data to put in those studies?

Basically, I solicit the data from certified business intermediaries. That's a designation given by the IBBA. I should mention that the business broker arena ranges from part-timers to those who possibly sell real estate and do maybe one or two transactions a year, to the brokers and intermediaries who are full-time professionals and have gone the extra step of becoming certified. I only include deals brokered by certified business intermediaries in order to make sure that the data they have supplied to us is reasonably consistent in terms of definitions of terminology.

BIZCOMPS is unique in that it doesn't provide the name of the target or acquiring company. Why is that?

Most people are familiar with comparatives, or "comps," in the context of real estate. In real estate, because you are dealing with real property, you're required by law to report the sales data. So, it's possible to go down to the County Recorder's office and find out what the person next door to you paid for the home they're in.

With businesses that aren't publicly traded, you're really just selling personal—or private—property. It's the same as selling somebody a table or a desk. All you give them is a bill of sale, and there's no requirement that the information be made public. The only people entitled to know the terms of the transaction are the buyer and seller, plus the intermediary when one is involved. However, in many cases, the intermediary has permission to disclose some or all aspects of the deal.

Is it difficult getting the intermediary to divulge the financial information to you for the BIZCOMPS studies?

I have what I feel is a win-win arrangement with them, which is simply that I give them a free copy of the current study for every ten transactions they provide. That's the best way to do it; I can't really buy data since that would taint its validity. On the other side of the coin, BIZCOMPS is valuable to brokers, and offering them a free study is a good way to encourage them to submit their information.

To answer your question, though, it *is* difficult to get the data from them simply because they're very time-constrained like everybody else. So, I just have to pester them and hope that they contribute when they can.

How do you address the issue of the credibility of the data, since it is self-reported?

Because it's provided by certified business intermediaries, number one. Number two, I look at all the data and I enter it personally myself, and have done that since day one. If something seems to be out of line or not normal, I will either call to try to find out more details, or I'll simply discard it.

Thirdly, if you are looking at enough data, there is a normalizing effect. In other words, if you're looking at thirty transactions, we know that statistically there's going to be something like five percent on each end of a bell curve that are sort of erratic. Then there's going to be some amount of normalcy among the rest of the data in the central part of that curve. In fact, it is fairly reliable.

One other reason is that all the data that I collect is the result of an asset sale. Asset sales are preferred because they limit contingent liability, such as liability passing from seller to buyer. If the data was from a stock sale, I find out enough information to convert it to an asset sale on paper, and discard items that cannot be converted to a normal asset sale. An asset sale generally comprises only fixtures and equipment and goodwill. In addition, inventory is either included or excluded. No other assets or liabilities are included.

What are the main reasons the owner of a small company decides to sell?

I have some ideas about that. I think that in the United States we tend to turn businesses over every five to eight years—although, in the fifteen years I've been doing this work, I have occasionally run into a business that somebody's had for ten or twenty years or even longer. But the majority of businesses are owned for five to eight years, and somewhere in that time period the business owner starts to burn out.

Another reason that is probably more fundamental is that small businesses have difficulty financing their growth internally over a long period of time, because there are very few sources of capital available to them. If you have good credit, you can borrow on a short-term basis to finance working capital. But in the long term, there are really not many ways of financing the growth of a business. That means that growth has to be achieved at the expense of the owner's profits. So, quite often, you'll see a business that is almost upside-down: They have way more debt than they should, simply because it's accumulated over a long period of time. That becomes uncomfortable for the seller, because they don't think they can retire the debt, and they don't want to cut their own wages. So, they put the business on the market. In comes a new buyer who will pay off the debts, which will be adjusted in the purchase price, and the business is recapitalized with the new buyer's funds.

Have you noticed in your experience that large publicly traded firms will come in and buy smaller companies?

Very rarely. Unfortunately, most large companies want to acquire firms that are doing at least $50 million in sales, if not more, in order to make the acquisition worth their while. You'd think that they'd want to grab a real bargain for $1 or $2 million, but frankly, it's not of much interest to them.

What is your relationship with NVST.com, and why did you decide to make BIZCOMPS available through them?

I see myself as a collector of the data, someone who keeps it organized and in the pipeline. But I am not really the vendor, or the person who wants to interface with the public and get it on the street. So, we sell BIZCOMPS through NVST.com, John Wiley and Sons [86], Practitioners Publishing Company [120], Pratt's Stats, and Moneyzone.com [104]. Also, the National Association of Certified Valuation Analysts [106] offers it on an individual, per-search basis.

Has the Internet increased the use of BIZCOMPS?

Yes. In the past I had to market BIZCOMPS by direct mailings and making personal presentations at conferences. The Internet allows much broader and more instantaneous use than the hard-copy studies. Users have more flexibility in their searches. And we are saving trees.

Do you recommend the Internet for any aspect of finding information on deals?

On appraisal assignments, I have the same problem as everyone else, in that I need to find market transactions. I look at IBA's database, Pratt's Stats, and Mergerstat [101]. Now, all of these databases are available on the Internet. I think the Internet is going to become more and more important as a transaction data source because, one day soon, there will be a Web site that allows you to search all the transaction databases at once.

Would you recommend that someone who is trying to find more information about the sale of a business call the broker?

When the broker's identity is available, that person is an excellent source of information about the details and motivations of a transaction.

As someone who compiles studies of transaction data, do you have any general advice for someone who looks for this data?

Transaction data represents averages. In addition to the data, researchers need to look more closely to compare the transaction data to the business they are trying to apply it to. For that reason, at BIZCOMPS we now provide twenty different parameters that define the transaction. We provide not only the company's SIC codes, but also information on the amount of equipment utilized, the amount of inventory they carry, the amount of rent paid, the number of days the business was on the market, and so on. These parameters can help you compare the deal with the company you are representing and determine why they might be more or less comparable.

Super Searcher Power Tips

➤ The BIZCOMPS studies are useful because they contain sales data for mom-and-pop-type businesses.

➤ Data provided by certified businesses intermediaries, as opposed to those who don't have the professional designation, tends to be more credible.

➤ Calling the person who brokered the deal is an excellent way of finding out additional information.

➤ You need to look at enough transaction data to be able to make averages, and then you need to ask questions beyond the data itself.

Rob Schlegel

Business Appraiser

Rob Schlegel is a business appraiser and principal with Houlihan Valuation Advisors in Indianapolis, Indiana.

robschlegel@hotmail.com
www.houlihan.com

Rob, tell me a bit about your background and the type of work you do.

I'm a principal with Houlihan Valuation Advisors, which is one of the national business valuation firms. We receive assignments that relate to everything from mergers and acquisitions, to economic studies, to estate and gift matters, to matrimonial divorce issues. But basically, we're business appraisers. In terms of my background, I suppose that I'm no more unique than most of the folks in this line of work. Our backgrounds tend to be a bit eclectic. I'm an economist; my master's degree is in labor and industrial relations, and my doctoral work was in management. I've spent time not only in the military, doing data processing kinds of things, but also as a college instructor. I've also led consulting practices for CPA firms.

I heard you speak at an Institute of Business Appraisers [75, see Appendix A] conference on

the various sources of M&A transaction data. Why do you use these types of data?

It's important to use transaction data because they provide solid evidence of market patterns and dynamics. In business valuation work, you have various standards of value. The most commonly used standard is fair market value, or the hypothetical exchange between a willing buyer and a willing seller, with neither being under compulsion or duress and both having knowledge of relevant facts. With that kind of standard, it's important that you understand what's happening in the market for this type of business or similar types of businesses. Transactional data is important evidence of the kinds of exchanges that have been done for businesses similar to the one that you're studying.

Also, keep in mind that valuation work does focus on a specific date. In other words, M&A work is normally focused on the here and now. What is this business worth *today* to a potential buyer? But you also have situations, such as a divorce, an economic study, or an estate tax issue when somebody passes away, where the value date will be sometime in the past. In the last two years, we've had assignments that go back 15 to 20 years. From that perspective, you do need to go back and research transactional evidence and economic evidence that existed as of the date of value.

So, the transaction data help you determine the value of a business?

They're certainly very strong indications. When you classify businesses, you look for the similarity of characteristics. If your selection of comparable businesses have similar market conditions, and you have transaction data, you have fairly strong evidence that the deal price of a business would be worth a multiple of earnings or revenues, or assets, or book value.

Let's start with those historical valuations. Where do you find information on the deals that occurred fifteen years ago?

That's a hard question because there aren't many sources. Probably the best database, going back to the mid-1980s, is the Institute of Business Appraisers (IBA) database of small transactions. In fact, they have data that go back into the early '70s. There are many other sources of transactional data in books, like the *Mergers & Acquisitions Sourcebook*. [99]

Do you use any magazines that report deals?

I've used the monthly journal *Mergers & Acquisition*s [98], and I've also used industry magazines. For example, say you are valuing an agricultural chemical manufacturer, and the date of value is 1980. It would make some sense to go back and find the industry magazines from that time period. Very often, the industry magazines will have articles that discuss, for instance, an annual convention. There are people who might have spoken at that convention 20 years ago, who still might be around, that you could phone. That type of research is really only limited by the type of lightbulb that you can turn on over your head.

Has the telephone approach worked well for you?

The phone is one thing that you can't escape. Most of the database information is sketchy at best. Because information is provided in summary form only, you may or may not have evidence of who the buyer or seller was. You might find yourself going to a library first to get a 1970 directory to find out where this business was located and get a phone number and do some tracking. But you certainly do pick up the phone and call. I've called chief financial officers of companies that have acquired other companies with the hope of finding out more information about a deal. It's not perfect information, and sometimes they just say, "I'm sorry, it's confidential." But many other times they say, "Of course, Rob, let me help you out. Here are the basic parameters that we looked for."

Where do you look for current deal information?

There are five databases that we use. I'll go through them in sort of random order. One is called DoneDeals [46], which is put together by the World M&A Network [162] out of Washington, DC, and was recently acquired by NVST.com [111]. A second source is Pratt's Stats [121; now Business Valuation Resources], a third one is BIZCOMPS [16], a fourth one is the IBA database that I previously mentioned, and the fifth one is Mergerstat [101]. Mergerstat also publishes books that contain M&A data, in addition to their database. It's important for researchers to understand that, in order to gain access to the IBA database, one either has to pay a fee per request or become a member of the organization. In fact, many associate members join the IBA simply to get access to the database. These are the five basic transactional databases that exist from a business appraisal standpoint.

Do you search all five of these databases for every assignment you work on?

For most clients, I would say that we might touch all of them, but it would be very rare to find any client situation where each of these data sources would be equally useful. You see, these databases come in different flavors—each one has its own strengths and weaknesses.

Can you give an example of when you would use Mergerstat instead of BIZCOMPS?

BIZCOMPS reports transactions from business brokers. Acquired companies with revenues of $500,000 to $1 or $2 million would be the common size of company you'd find in BIZ-COMPS. Mergerstat, on the other hand, contains transactions of companies much greater in size. Mergerstat picks up public information that's reported to them from the large investment banks, press releases, and industry news. I believe they also check U.S. Securities and Exchange Commission [152] (SEC) filings for transactions. So, the small transaction of a dry cleaner sold to some other dry cleaner in East Weed, Indiana, might be reported in BIZCOMPS, but it probably wouldn't be in Mergerstat.

The size of the company that you're valuing, then, would determine which database you use?

Yes, that's one important criteria. DoneDeals is a compendium of deals that are reported to the SEC by publicly traded companies—what we call material transactions. DoneDeals began in the mid-1990s, but it became much more useful in '96 and '97 when the size of the database grew. Because it is based on deals reported to the SEC, DoneDeals tends to contain mid-market acquisitions, valued at several million dollars up to $100 million and more. I have found that most of the transactions tend to cluster around $5, $10, $15 million, and the majority are acquisitions of privately held companies. That's the flavor of DoneDeals.

What about Pratt's Stats? That's a relatively new database also, isn't it?

Dr. Shannon Pratt, whom the business valuation community considers its guru by most accounts, established Pratt's Stats several years ago. He and his staff are judiciously gathering information from business brokers and organizations that will share detailed financial information about transactions. The advantage of Pratt's Stats is that it provides a great deal of financial analysis based on the balance sheets and income statements, as well as terms of the transactions. Pratt's Stats probably has more raw data associated with each transaction than any of the other sources I've mentioned. On the other hand, because it's relatively new, Pratt's Stats is strong in data from the last two or three years, but I don't think you should depend on it for deals done in the mid-'90s.

Do you use any other sources that we haven't talked about?

In terms of business valuation, there is probably no limit to the number of sources you might use. The common joke in the industry is that it's easy to get into the business of valuing companies, except when you realize that you have to spend $5,000 to $10,000 to start a library.

One book we frequently use is the *Business Reference Guide* [21], published by the Business Brokerage Press. It's actually a compendium edited by Tom West, who is very well-known in business broker circles. The nice thing about the *Business Reference Guide* is that it talks about how deals are done and provides hundreds of references in terms of whom to call and where to look on the Internet for more information. But the most important aspect of the *Guide* are the rules of thumb it provides. Let's suppose we're valuing a convenience store. The *Guide* has a one-half page summary of rules of thumb on convenience stores in terms of value, for instance, the industry's multiple is 10 to 22 percent of gross sales, or four to six times cash flow.

It is important to keep in mind, when you use these rules of thumb, that you're usually talking about a deal price, which is fixed assets plus goodwill in a very general sense but does not include cash, real estate, liabilities, or other things that are inside a business's balance sheet. Also keep in mind that there can be a lot of confusion in terms of exactly what is being sold. Are you selling the stock or are you just selling selected assets, such as all the furniture and tables and chairs plus the goodwill? You have to make sure you understand what you're talking about in any given transaction. The *Business Reference Guide* is a wonderful sanity check because it provides general rules of thumb, but it's not something on which you would typically base final calculations without further analysis.

We also use a series called *The Mergers and Acquisitions Sourcebook*, which was prepared by Walter Jurick and the Quality Services Company [126]. The *Sourcebook* contains fairly good deal summaries, comes out on an annual basis, and is organized by industry. Dr. Jurick also published *Business Valuations by Industry* [22], which provides more in-depth analyses of particular industries, and the *Corporate Growth Report* [38], which gives detailed information about particular acquisitions. I believe that NVST.com recently acquired the rights to all these publications and will be publishing them from now on.

Yes, NVST.com has bought DoneDeals and the Quality Services publications. Do you ever use NVST.com for M&A research?

As a matter of fact, we do. NVST.com is a dot-com company that is becoming, for many of us, the clearinghouse for information relating to business valuation. DoneDeals and BIZ-COMPS are accessible through the site. NVST.com provides links to just about every M&A-related organization around, such as the Association for Corporate Growth [13]. And if you want to subscribe to publications such as *Buyouts* [24] or *Mergers & Acquisitions*, you can do so through the site and receive the articles online.

You mentioned the need to know the details of a deal, such as whether it's a stock deal. Do all of the databases provide that information?

DoneDeals, Mergerstat, and Pratt's Stats will indicate if it is an asset deal or a stock deal. With BIZCOMPS, the presumption is that the deals are asset deals or, in other words, goodwill plus fixed assets. However, you need to be careful how you use the raw data because, if you mix these apples and oranges, you can arrive at an entirely wrong result. Consequently, you may have to make some accounting adjustments. This is why those who tend to be more successful and prominent in the industry have some background in accounting and finance.

Would you ever use the EDGAR [51] database to try to find more information about a deal?

Sure. If the deal is big enough, it may be filed with the SEC. In that case, you could look into FreeEDGAR [59] or one of the other EDGAR sites to see what has been reported. DoneDeals and Mergerstat will also reflect some of the SEC data, but you may want to go back into EDGAR to find out more of the deal's background. You might also look in Dun & Bradstreet's *Million Dollar Directory* [103], not for the transaction, but to find out the name of the company and its officers, in order to make a phone call. Standard & Poor's [141], typically found in your local public library, is a good source for finding information on publicly traded companies.

Are there any other Internet sites that you use for M&A research?

There's a ton of them! The one that I probably use most is called DailyStocks.com [40], because it is sort of a funnel site that provides links to hundreds of other sources. On DailyStocks I can search by an Standard Industrial Classification (SIC) code, the name of a company, or a geographic area, and do research from the links that the site provides. Granted, much of the financial information pertains to publicly traded companies, but you can also find good industry data. Even though a small, privately held company may be the subject of your research, it's nonetheless important to understand the general trends and dynamics of the industry group to which it belongs. Let's take a look at how the nursing home industry, for example, has fared from 1997 forward. You may find that the bottom has fallen out in the past 24 months. That's the kind of research that's available on DailyStocks.

What are some of the challenges and pitfalls in doing transaction research?

The realization that you can never do enough research and that you have to make decisions based on imperfect information. The search for transactional evidence is bounded by certain factors aside from the availability of information, such as the time available, the budget that you have, the efficiency with which you approach the job, and the wisdom with which you gather industry or specific company information. You have to do the best you can with the resources available.

Another pitfall is that you probably can never get enough transactional evidence on a specific deal. You may be able to get the financials, and you may be able to talk to people about the deal, but there may be important facts that, regardless of your diligence, you miss.

Do you mean proprietary knowledge?

Sure. Say, for example, you have a transaction involving a company in Cleveland, Ohio, that seems to have a little lower price than normal. You'd probably want to find out why. It could be because a competitor just built a factory across the street, or because the management team suffered from some grievous loss. You have these unique aspects that are really hard to ferret out. That's one of the reasons why there is a benefit in larger sample numbers. The more you get, looking at the means and the medians—medians are more normal than means—the better. Then, looking at the trends, you have more confidence in the numbers. If you base decisions on just one or two individual transactions, you're much more vulnerable to being surprised because of some fact or facet that you didn't know.

Do you find that research is complicated by the fact there is often too much data available?

With the Internet, there's tons and tons of information out there. Much of it is good but not for your particular project. There's a lot of incorrect stuff out there, too. But you would be surprised at what you can find by looking into, for example, competitor companies' Web sites. You can pick up aspects that give you tremendous amounts of insight into how the competitors of your subject or target company view the industry.

Are there any words of wisdom you'd like to share about doing this type of research?

I have three suggestions. My first suggestion is to make sure that you understand the trends in the industry in which the company you are researching operates and the economic trends in the time period that you're researching. This is absolutely vital, and it is above and beyond simple transactional research. The transactions tend to vary according to certain characteristics. When times are flush and good, the transactions would tend to show a higher value or multiple. When times are bad, it may be the other way. You'll find noticeable trends, for example, in software companies or Internet companies when the market gets saturated or when it's hungry.

The second suggestion is to make sure that you understand what's going on in the geography, or the regional territory of the company that you're researching. Each company obviously is unique, but they have supplier chains, customer bases, limits on their human resources, and they may be buffeted by other economic changes in their home territory or region.

The third suggestion relates to competitive intelligence. Make sure that you do enough background research surrounding the issue at hand. While researching the environment of a transaction, you may find out things about a company that the management of that company may not even know. Think of it as dropping a pebble in a pool of water and seeing the expanding rings. You need to go out three or four rings each time you're doing this kind of research.

Super Searcher Power Tips

➤ Industry publications can be a great source of M&A information.

➤ You can't escape the phone—you'll need it to find out additional information.

➤ Very often, the industry magazines from 20 years ago will have articles that discuss, for instance, an annual convention. There are people who might have spoken at that convention, who still might be around, that you could phone.

➤ As a business appraiser, I use five different databases for transactional data. Each one has its own strengths and weaknesses.

➤ While the *Business Reference Guide* is a wonderful sanity check, it's not something on which you would typically base final calculations.

➤ DoneDeals and Mergerstat reflect some SEC data, but you may want to go into EDGAR to find out more of the deal's background.

Ed Vazquez

M&A Database Product Developer

At the time of this interview, Ed Vazquez was senior product manager with Data Downlink, producer of xls.com and Portal B. He is now senior product manager with Inlumen, Inc.

evazquez@inlumen.com
www.inlumen.com

Ed, can you tell me about your M&A research experience?

I've had a pretty interesting background. I started right out of library school working at an investment bank called Lazard Frères, where I was under the tutelage of Anne Mintz. I went on to work at another investment bank, Morgan Stanley, and then at an M&A boutique, the Bridgeford Group, where I worked very closely with the investment bankers. I ended up with Wasserstein Perella, where I was the manager of information services. It was a great job because I had a lot of close ties with the bankers and helped them complete some major M&A deals. So, I've been in the finance end of librarianship for about ten of the fifteen years I've been working in libraries.

Let's talk a little bit about the M&A research you did for the bankers. Was it pretty much the same type of research at each of the banks you worked for?

The research was usually the "full-blast" approach, which entailed scouring an industry to identify potential targets for some of the firm's buyers. This type of research, where we're trying to identify candidates for potential acquisition, doesn't usually require the M&A transaction databases as much as it does the news and directory-type databases.

So a banker would come to you and say "I need to identify some possible acquisition candidates in XYZ industry?"

Exactly. We'd begin this kind of research with the traditional reference interview because bankers often make somewhat vague requests, like "I'm interested in sunglass companies." So, we'd ask: Sunglass manufacturers or retailers? What is the size of the company we're looking for? Is there a geographic location that's preferable? Are we looking for a particular type of management style? Do we want to find public companies or private companies? Once we've narrowed the scope of the search, we are able to come up with a list of what they call their top-tier candidates.

Sounds like the reference interview is pretty important.

We really needed to get the gist of what they were looking for. Otherwise, we'd waste a lot of time, and we didn't have any time to waste.

Did you use both print and online sources?

To identify companies, we'd use the traditional directory databases that contain elaborate business descriptions. It was usually better to search the business descriptions as opposed to the Standard Industrial Classification (SIC) codes. If you're looking for companies that make sunglasses, there isn't a specific enough SIC code. It is easier to find useful business descriptions in databases of publicly traded companies, such as Standard and Poor's [141, see Appendix A] or Market Guide [95], rather than databases like Dun & Bradstreet [49]. Because Dun & Bradstreet contains so many privately held companies, it can only provide a few descriptive words for each business.

We'd then come up with our top-tier list, as well as second- and third-tier lists of candidates. But we would try to get as much information as possible on the top-tier candidates.

What type of information would you provide on your top-tier list candidates?

We would try to get the inside scoop on these companies. We'd take a look at their Web sites, find news and journal articles, and get the necessary Securities and Exchange Commission (SEC) documents if they were publicly traded.

Were you selective in what you handed over to the bankers, or did they want to see everything? In other words, did you provide any value-added services, like highlighting the pertinent parts?

Where information specialists really add value is in their experience—knowing where to turn for the answer to the question. This happens at the moment the reference interview is completed. Selecting the right sources from the start of a search is critical. It saves time and money. Although money is usually not the determining factor, time is valuable to a banker working on a project. If an online service costs more but provides the answer in a timely manner, we would select that one. Bankers are less concerned with expenses since they feel their time is valuable, and they can pass along the expenses to the client.

What happened after the banker reviewed the top-tier list?

The banker would decide which company to pursue, and then conduct a valuation to determine how much it would probably cost to acquire the company.

Did the bankers come back to you for more information in order to prepare the valuation?

Yes, we would do searches on Securities Data Company's (SDC) Worldwide M&A Database [163] to find comparable transactions and their multiples. Although bankers rely on their own analysis, we would supplement it with SDC data. However, the multiples that SDC provides are used as a guide and never taken as gospel. Bankers, as fiduciaries, have a responsibility to their clients to run the numbers themselves and not take a third party's interpretation.

So, you'd identify possible acquisition clients, find background information on them, and locate comparable acquisitions. What other types of research did you do?

We worked the other side of the fence as well. If one of the bank's clients wanted to sell a sunglass manufacturer, then we'd sort of do the reverse. We would identify potential buyers, like optical manufacturers, and put those companies in a tier class as well. Then we'd eventually search SDC for comparable transactions.

How would you find what companies were on the acquisition trail, so to speak?

Company press releases will often state that the company has taken on a strategic advisor, or has just hired a banker. This is usually an indication either that something's for sale or they're looking to buy something. Or companies will announce that they're looking for strategic alternatives. Or they'll flat out mention that they are selling a business.

So, we would search press releases using certain keywords and phrases, like "seeking strategic alternatives" or "hires banker." We'd also set up alerts on databases for press releases that used these keywords, so that we could inform a banker of a potential project. The alerts served as a prospecting tool.

What were your favorite online databases for press releases and alerts?

Desktop Data's NewsEdge [110] and Dow Jones Interactive [54] Clip are two services we used to alert us to potential business. NewsEdge's real-time news feeds were monitored up to the minute by library staff. The banker acted on any potential lead immediately.

Let's switch gears. Now you're on the other side of the fence, the data provider side. How was that transition made and why did you decide to do it?

That was an interesting turn of events. The President and CEO of Data Downlink [43] were developing an idea for a product that would leverage their current collection of services, namely financial, quantitative-type databases. They found that a lot of their customers were using their databases for quantitative information, but that they also used the Web for additional business research. They realized that a lot of librarians were maintaining and using Web site bookmarks in lieu of search engines because the search engines were often cumbersome when doing business research.

When I was at Wasserstein Perella, I maintained a collection of 1,500 bookmarks that I used all the time. If I was working on a project involving the insurance industry, I would go to my "insurance" bookmarks as a way of starting my research. Building the bookmark collection was a tedious process, but it turned out to be very worthwhile because I could actually go directly to a great source and find what I needed, instead of going off to the major search engines and doing a full-blast search.

So, Data Downlink had an idea to create a fully integrated business information portal for research professionals. I was hired by them to work on the product. It's called Portal B [118]. It became commercially available in May of 2000.

Was your encyclopedic-size bookmark file part of the reason they hired you?

Well, that and my contacts and experience of course!

Tell me more about Portal B.

We took those 1,500 bookmarks and the bookmarks from some other librarians who maintain similar business-related bookmark collections, as well as those from other Web sites that maintain collections, and we created a single mega-database of trade associations, trade publications, business magazines, business schools, law firms, law schools, and government sites. We compiled all the URLs into a database and added some controlled vocabulary and indexing. The site is categorized along industry, subject, and geographic lines, and you can actually search the full text of each site. The database now has approximately 8,500 business-oriented sites, handpicked by information professionals.

The exciting aspect of Portal B is that we spider each of the sites in our mega-database, including PDF documents at the site. We simultaneously search the Web sites and the premium content that we license. So, when users search our collection of Web sites for information, they simultaneously search our premium content. A flag will come up indicating that data is available within our collection of premium databases. It's not obtrusive or forced on the user.

I'm curious how Portal B relates to fee-based databases like Mergerstat [101]. Say I'm

looking at an industry—equipment rental, for example—that has experienced a lot of consolidation. How will information on this subject be flagged to transactions in Mergerstat?

Conceivably, if you search Portal B by company name and matches are found in Mergerstat or Securities Data, there'll be a little flag that says "XYZ is identified in Mergerstat, there's data available, and this is how much it will cost."

I'm looking forward to checking out Portal B. What a great way to take the knowledge you've learned from your years in investment banks and apply it to a new product.

It's a culmination of fifteen years as an information professional. It has been a rewarding project because it has given me an opportunity to create something to help my colleagues tame the Web. It's a tool that will really assist in the research process.

Tell me more about the two well-known M&A databases available from Data Downlink— Mergerstat and SDC's Worldwide M&A Database.

Mergerstat and SDC are the premier sources for M&A transaction data. The two products have interesting histories. Mergerstat began as a print publication some thirty-five years ago. W.T. Grimm published the printed source for several years. Merrill Lynch bought it and subsequently sold it to Houlihan Lukey Howard & Zukin, a middle market investment bank. They finally turned it into a commercially available electronic database. Renowned for its M&A statistics, Mergerstat can now leverage its advantage to compete with SDC.

Securities Data Company, on the other hand, has provided M&A data in electronic format since the early '80s, and has had the luxury of being "the" authority on M&A transaction data. It is widely used by every major investment bank and supplements its database with additional, related financial data on the same platform. The platform has never been the easiest to use and has only recently been made available through a Web interface by Data Downlink Corporation. In fact, Data Downlink offers both MergerStat and SDC on the same service—it is unique, in this day and age, to offer competing products under the same umbrella.

Aside from the Mergerstat and the SDC databases, what other mergers and acquisitions-related databases are on Data Downlink's .xls [165] service?

The Carson Group [25] and the Vickers Stock Research [156] databases provide ownership information on public companies. You could conceivably identify individuals or institutions that own a significant stake in target companies. The banker could approach the owner and pursue a private purchase of these stakes in order to gain a minority or controlling interest in the company, without having to launch a public takeover of a private company.

The other M&A database on the .xls service that is useful for doing this type of research is Securities Data Joint Venture Database [87]. With this database, a banker can identify when two parties have gotten together in the past, and might surmise that it makes sense to approach them with a similar venture or acquisition candidate.

At Data Downlink, do you ever get feedback from the public about other types of M&A-related information they want?

One piece of the puzzle that has been very hard for people to find is the whole area of private equity ownership of a company. For example, M&A bankers have a difficult time discovering what private equity firms have in their collections of portfolio companies. These firms usually take a minority stake, sometimes even a controlling stake, in a company in order to turn it around and sell it at a premium somewhere down the road. Many of these private equity companies don't have Web sites, and they don't want to be bothered putting up Web sites because they're too busy making money. So, it's hard to find out what these companies are up to. In Portal B, we've included the top 250 private equity firms that have Web sites. Many of these sites list the company's portfolios. Not only can you get a directory listing of all these firms, but you can search the content of their Web sites as well.

Does the fact that so many private equity firms do not have Web sites mean that it is a secretive industry?

I don't really think it's secretive. I think they just haven't had time to create a presence on the Web. In most cases, they *want* bankers to know that they own a stake in a company because they want the bankers to come up with an offer. Many of the firms are now realizing that the Web is actually a very good way of promoting their portfolios. For example, if you go to the Web site for Flatiron Partners [58], a firm that owns a stake in Data Downlink, you will find a list of all the investments they've made, which of those have been sold, which have gone public, and so on. In fact, many companies that are part of a portfolio really want to have their private equity firms announce that they own a stake. This is especially true now, with all the venture-backed Internet companies, because they all want to go public and they all want to get bought so their options can kick in.

It sounds like the Internet has made it possible for researchers to find more information on private equity firms.

Absolutely. In the past, obtaining their portfolio information was very difficult. They'd publish brochures or leave stuff out on their coffee tables, but there was no vehicle to get at this type of information in a systematic way. One had to contact the company to ask if they had anything for sale, or anything in their portfolio of investments that was ready to be turned around.

Is there anything else on the M&A databases wish list?

A couple of databases out there are attempting to put together a list of companies owned by these private equity groups. Securities Data is trying to do one called Venture Expert, but I think they're missing the boat because they're just looking at venture-backed companies. There are really two aspects of that coin: the venture-backed companies and the private equity companies. Venture databases assist in the M&A process by identifying companies that are seeking capital, which may be an indicator to a potential sale of a company down the road. The databases are incomplete because the data is compiled from surveys, and companies often are just too busy to answer the survey.

What do you read to keep current?

Many things. *The Wall Street Journal* [157], of course. *Online* [114], *EContent* [50], *Information Today* [72], and *Information World Review* [73]. But many of the publications I read are electronic, like Danny Sullivan's *Search Engine Watch* [130], Greg Notess' *Search Engine Showdown* [129], Free Pint [60], CNET Tech News [30], and CNET Finance and Investing [29]. I'm really a sponge when it comes to information that affects what I do for a living.

Do you participate in any electronic mailing lists or discussion groups?

For what I do, the best list of all is Buslib-L [23]. It is just great for hearing what's on librarians' minds and what they are working on. I love supplying answers to questions and being acknowledged for it.

I also subscribe to my alma mater's listserv. St. John's University's Division of Library Science posts information that is important to me as an alumnus and as an adjunct professor. It's great for leads on information initiatives that the school is undertaking.

What advice would you give someone who wants to be an expert M&A researcher?

You know, you can be the best librarian or best researcher in the world, but you still need to understand the business. You need to get into the heads of bankers to find out why they're looking for this information, why they *need* this information. It's good to understand the process, to make the research more effective. And that's not a very easy thing to do.

How did you do it? Did you have a business background besides your library degree?

Not at all. You just have to be interested and patient and ask questions. I was a communications major as an undergrad. I really got exposed to the business while working at a small M&A boutique, where I had to wear several hats and was involved in the whole process. I was invited to one series of meetings because we had a potential client who was a commercial information vendor looking to sell part of his business. As the expert on commercial information services, I was called into the meetings and the bankers would ask, "What do you think of this company's service? Do you think it's worth anything?"

Do you think that working at a smaller firm, where the bankers are more willing to explain things, would help someone who is just starting out as a business and finance librarian?

Yes. I was fortunate enough to be a part of the firm's meetings where I would discuss the latest additions on our intranet. But I made a point of sticking around for the rest of the meeting and listening to what was going on and what people were working on. I got a head start on what kind of research would be coming in to the information center. But it's truly a matter of listening to what the bankers are asking and knowing why they need it. It's always difficult to get all the answers from the bankers, but eventually you'll put the pieces together.

Super Searcher Power Tips

➤ To identify companies, we'd use the traditional directory databases that contain elaborate business
descriptions. It is usually better to search the business
descriptions as opposed to the SIC codes.

➤ Where information specialists really add value is in
their experience—knowing where to turn for the
answer to the question. This happens at the moment
the reference interview is completed. Selecting the
right sources from the start of a search is critical. It
saves time and money.

➤ We would do searches on SDC's Worldwide M&A
Database to find comparable transactions and their
multiples. However, the multiples that SDC provides
are used as a guide and never taken as gospel.
Bankers, as fiduciaries, have a responsibility to their
clients to run the numbers themselves and not take a
third party's interpretation.

➤ You can be the best librarian or researcher in the
world, but you still need to understand the business.
You need to get into the heads of bankers to find out
why they're looking for this information, why they
need this information. I made a point of listening to
what was going on and what people were working on.

Bruce Liebman

Librarian and Information Professional

Bruce Liebman is the Senior Information Specialist at Houlihan Lokey Howard & Zukin, a specialty investment bank. After several years in the trenches assisting bankers on Wall Street, Bruce is now assisting them in sunny Southern California.

bliebman@hlhz.com
www.hlhz.com

Bruce, would you tell me a little about your background?

When I was a young tyke, I was a clerk in the fact-checking department of the semi-world-renowned Time, Inc. editorial library. I bounced between there and the *Sports Illustrated* library. This was 1981 or '82, before computers really took over everything. At Time, I was in line to move up to the *Sports Illustrated* library, which was one of the best-known sports libraries in the country. But it wasn't exactly what I wanted to do with my life at that age. I really had my heart set on being a general fact-checker for all the Time, Inc. publications; I looked up to those professionals so much. As a perk, Time paid for me to go to library school, and I thought "why not?" I figured that I should get ahead of the curve for once, and if they were paying for me to go to library school to be a reference guru, I couldn't lose.

What library school did you attend?

Columbia. What really opened my eyes in library school was online research, and how everything was moving online. I was fascinated with being able to do research electronically. But thank God I had a little bit of grounding in traditional classic reference from the well-known professors at Columbia. By classic reference, I mean the standard print sources for the sciences and the humanities. You really should know the standard bibliographies, encyclopedias, and directories. Maybe Microsoft has put them all on CD-ROM by now, but at that time computers were not yet on the academic's desktop.

At that point, my tastes in research got more catholic. When I was in the sixth grade, my teacher said that my reading tastes were "not very catholic." He meant I should get my head out of the sports world and into anything else. I always kept that suggestion in my head when I worked at *Sports Illustrated*. After library school, I worked in the law library at the Court of International Trade. It used to be called the U.S. Customs Court; I don't know what it's called now. That job was as dry as dust—researching import/export disputes and tariff cases. I left after a year. I wanted to go into business research, because it was by far my favorite course at Columbia.

Then in late 1984, I applied for a part-time job at Merrill Lynch on the investment banking side. Merrill Lynch was well-known for its retail operations, and that group had its own library that operated nine to five. But the investment banking information center was separate and wanted to extend its hours into the early evening. I was a single guy at the time and they needed someone to come in to do online reference in the evening. So, along with Brian Gallagher at Salomon Brothers, I was one of the pioneers of the late shift in Wall Street libraries in the mid-'80s. This job was a real trial by fire for me because I was new and still learning. But the four women on the staff were so happy that somebody was working the night shift that they took me under their wings. They taught me the basics of online databases and what we call "meatball reference."

Meatball reference?

You know, questions like "just give me everything on this company back a hundred years." I had a friend at library school who had a similar job at one of the other top firms on Wall Street. I saw her at a function and she said, "I hate it, it's all meatball reference." Some people call it "quick-and-dirty" reference. Anyway, after two years, Merrill hired me full-time, and I worked a very difficult shift, from one until nine p.m. We ended up hiring five more people in '87. So, by then, I was working more regular hours.

Were you busy up until nine o'clock at night?

Pretty much. It slowed down at the dinner hour, but there were certainly enough requests to keep us busy.

What were your typical requests, other than meatball reference questions? What would these bankers want at nine o'clock at night?

We would tend to get into meatball reference during the very early morning hours and the very late hours. "Who owns the stock?" "Can I get news about the company?" "Can I have a list of their mergers?" They needed this information for due diligence, for prospecting, for comparison, who knows what. Now, in all the major investment banking information centers during this time, one-half of the library was set up to crank out SEC documents. We had a *very* large staff on the documents desk to print out SEC documents. This was before EDGAR [51, see Appendix A], you know.

What types of filings would you print out, and why?

It was always the big four document types—10-Ks, 10-Qs, prospectuses, proxies—because bankers have to ultimately check the original source documents. At the time, OneSource

[113] and Compustat [33] were available, but the numbers that those secondary sources provide need to be double-checked against the original SEC source documents. It was wild; you'd walk the halls and see piles and piles of SEC printouts. The bankers would have to go through everything in those documents—including the footnotes—with a fine-toothed comb.

Tell me more about Merrill Lynch's Information Center.

We had seven people on the reference staff, and each person had his or her own specialty or expertise. One person knew a lot about international companies and international documents, one person was strong in financial institutions, another person was strong in government documents and economics. I sort of fell into my specialty, which was general corporate finance. Often my research involved digging as far as I could to find information on a particular merger. A lot of times I would need to find empirical studies in databases like ABI Inform [2].

I have to tell you about the research the junior analysts had to do that involved the library. Every year they were given the same research assignment. It was always the same project. They'd be given lists with hundreds of company names, organized alphabetically. Each analyst would take a letter of the alphabet and research the companies whose names started with their letter. They'd have to find out things like "Which of the companies had cut their dividend?" So, these new analysts would come to the information center and have us run searches on Moody's [57] and Standard & Poor's [141], and print out the company name and the dividend change. Then they would go back to their spreadsheets and figure out the effect of the change on the stock price.

Bankers would also come into the information center, often with laundry lists of companies. They'd want to know everything about these companies, and we'd have to research one after the other. Every day the documents desk would get requests like "Get me all the merger prospecti for this deal." Unfortunately, about half the requests would come in with the company's name spelled wrong, or with a wrong date. So, at the end of the day, the document center would hand me a list of prospecti they could not find. Because I was the corporate finance specialist, I had to try to figure out which prospectus the banker really wanted. Until Bloomberg [17] arrived, that was a real pain.

Why did Bloomberg change that?

Bloomberg was partially owned by Merrill, and they built their prospectus collection from the Merrill Lynch prospectus collection, which was probably one of the deepest on Wall Street. Before the Bloomberg database, I had to hope to find terms of the deal in the Securities Data M&A database [148], the Moody's Manuals, or Disclosure [45]. Half the time, the documents that people wanted weren't in any of these sources because the target or acquiring company was privately held and didn't release any public documents. With a simple keystroke, Bloomberg would tell you whether the deal was public or private, thus saving a lot of time.

Did the arrival of EDGAR change that research process?

I left Merrill right before EDGAR hit the scene. But I do know that it didn't really change matters much from a research standpoint. With EDGAR, more people had immediate access to documents right from their desktops, but the needle-in-a-haystack problem remained.

What was your favorite type of research at Merrill Lynch?

My favorite research involved questions that required problem solving, like "I need to find companies that simultaneously did a stock split and an IPO." You can't answer that question with a database query. You have to rely on your smarts, figure out where the information might be published, or who you might call. I was always in contact with Moody's and S&P for help with those esoteric studies.

Also, the research department from the noninvestment banking side of the firm gave us very interesting research requests to work on—requests that *didn't* need turnover in an hour.

Once I worked with the head of Merrill Lynch's high-yield group, Martin Fridson. He was a top-ranked research director and very astute. He had me work on a very interesting study on the general legal treatment of companies that went into bankruptcy before, during, and after the Civil War. These types of projects were always gratifying because they made me think— made me go into areas I didn't know, try to uncover experts, and then beg, borrow, and plead to get information.

One time, for a creative outlet, I rebuilt part of our classic finance book collection. People would come to the information center and find that we didn't have the basic books, like one on how the bond and stock markets function. So, I set up a small special collection of the investment classics. I really enjoyed that, especially because I got to go to the used bookstores in New York to find them.

Why did you leave Merrill Lynch?

On Wall Street, you keep very long hours. I felt like I was burning out after almost ten years. There wasn't much creativity needed on most requests, and my reference skills were deteriorating because I was doing the same thing every day. My wife got into the MBA program at the University of Southern California; I'd always wanted to try California for a while. You know, the whole "reinventing of self" that Los Angeles represents.

Where did your career pick up in California?

On the reference desks of a couple of public libraries, including the Los Angeles Public Library. The LAPL has a big reference collection and research library, and I was able to work with a reference staff that had many years of experience solving a larger sphere of economics and finance questions. Having to deal with people one-on-one—most of the requests at Merrill came by phone or e-mail—I quickly discovered that the old reference interview was a skill set I definitely needed to improve.

How else did the public library environment differ from the investment bank environment?

People are much more grateful in a public setting. I wasn't used to people saying thank you. In both sectors, though, people usually don't want to read a 10-K because it's too much work. They want just a one-page sheet from *ValueLine* [153] or S&P. When I was working on a public reference desk, it was interesting to see people who really were persistent and would want you to download an EDGAR document for them in ASCII. But, although EDGAR increased the amount of information available, in my mind it didn't really change my business at all. People would still say, "I need to know who the board of directors are." They don't want to print out a huge document; they just want the answer.

Too often in the private sector, people not only want you to do the research, they want you to end up, almost, with the finished PowerPoint slide that they'll use in their presentation! When I was at Merrill, people would come down and ask for a kind of study that Moody's or S&P might have done. Once I said to an analyst: "What you want is somebody's preformatted study." He replied, "Yeah, that's right."

Tell me about the firm where you work now, Houlihan Lokey Howard & Zukin.

Houlihan Lokey is a specialty investment bank, with offices in the U.S. and Asia. The main difference between our firm and a Merrill Lynch, for example, is that we do not do any underwriting of securities. We primarily focus on middle market private companies. Middle market is usually defined as companies with less than $250 million in revenues. We do, however, help to arrange debt and equity financing as well as provide general corporate finance and merger and acquisition advisory services.

What's the typical sort of question an analyst will ask you?

I often put together buyers lists for the analysts. Say we have a client who has a company that operates in a new manufacturing niche, and he wants to sell it. We have to find all similar companies in that same market. This research is very time-consuming because we often come up with telephone-book-size lists.

Where do you start to pull together companies for a buyers list?

We search through all sorts of directory-type databases that contain public and private companies. We'd usually start with Compact Disclosure [31], S&P, and the various Dun & Bradstreet products on Dialog Corporation [44]. People in investment banking love any product with detailed business descriptions since that helps them more accurately pinpoint companies.

Do you ever use regional news databases or industry databases like PROMT [124]?

I don't search PROMT very much. I've been very frustrated with PROMT over the years. If I want to know the size of the doorknob industry in Senegal, it seems that I can find it in a second, but if I want to know the size of the same industry in the U.S., I just can't find it.

One source I really need on my desk at all times is Trip Wyckoff's *Special Issues* [135]. This directory, as well as Gale's *Encyclopedia of Business Information Sources* [53], lists the publications that produce buyer's guides. Buyer's guides are worth their weight in gold because they list hundreds of companies that relate in some aspect to a particular industry, and they are much more descriptive than D&B or S&P directories.

So, for instance, a trade publication like *Contractor* has a yearly Buyer's Guide that people can use to find a particular product or service?

Yes, and if I get my hands on one of those, I pass it on to the analyst and they just go to town. The top people are on the phone trying to find expressions of interest. Because those lists contain the *real* buyers.

Does the analyst or the banker depend on you to compile the ultimate buyers list?

No, because they have a lot of internal lists that are kept, fortunately, so that you don't have to reinvent the wheel every day. But generally we'll start with the client having some idea of what he or she is looking for. The analysts will search FactSet [55], Disclosure, or S&P for the larger public and private companies.

What does the final buyers list look like?

Fortunately, I don't have to put it together. That's why God invented analysts. They'll format about fifty companies per "book." For each company you'll find the name, location, sales, business description, and whether it's public or private. One of the good things about working with smaller companies is that they end up with smaller lists. When I was at Merrill, these lists would seem to go on forever.

Do the analysts ask you to find all the transactions in a particular industry?

Absolutely. If we're advising a company on a merger, we have to know about similar deals in order to know what the multiples are. It's multiple mania at all the investment firms. They always need to know things like what the "enterprise value"— basically the total value of a firm's debt and equity minus cash on the balance sheet—of a transaction was or what the price was as a percent of revenues, net income, or enterprise value.

I should say that Houlihan owns one of the key M&A transaction databases, Mergerstat [101]. It's a separate division, and now it's off-site. But, generally, the analysts at Houlihan Lokey have access to Mergerstat, and they do a lot of searching for deals on their own. Finding transactions can be difficult, because we always seem to be dealing with niche-type companies that are privately held. I always hope that the databases include the sales of the target company.

Other sources I rely on are three Dialog databases: Trade and Industry Database [149], File 148, Business and Industry [19], File 9, and Business Dateline [20], File 635. I don't want to show a preference for Dialog over Dow Jones Interactive [54] or Lexis-Nexis [90], but Dialog's indexing is so good. I also depend on *The Wall Street Journal* [157]. I use these sources for transaction searches because a magazine or newspaper sometimes makes a passing reference to the terms of a deal that will not be found in the merger databases.

One other database that I use extensively for industry overviews is ProQuest [125] on the Web. Rather than printing out reams of cites from all the traditional news vendors, one can go to ProQuest and get a facsimile of the actual article from leading industry publications. Before the Internet a product like that would have been unimaginable.

What other types of research projects do you work on?

We do research on the flip side of the coin as well: Who are the likely *sellers*? We work very closely with private equity firms that have portfolios of companies. It's like baseball cards; they buy them, they trade them, they flip them left and right. So, we look for expressions of interest in the private equity firms. We also use private equity and venture capital directories from firms such as Asset Alternatives [12] and SDC [148].

How often do you pick up the phone when a database doesn't provide what you need?

That's why you had trouble reaching me—I'm always on the phone! My philosophy is this: Collectively, investment banks spend hundreds of thousands of dollars on information products. Databases and such get you in the door, but the information is often incomplete. So, we have to pick up the phone and call whatever subject specialists we can find. Over time, you develop a feel for whether a particular factoid is likely to be available, which saves you a bit of online research time and money.

What are some examples of research projects where you've relied heavily on the phone?

I've been trying to get my hands on a bridge loan prospectus. This type of document is a highly confidential, Wall Street-type offering. Analysts like to look at a document's structure because it's a template for a similar document we may be creating.

So, you're basically trying to convince someone on the phone to send it to you?

If I already have a relationship with the person I'm calling, I have no compunction about asking for it for free. You know how it is; some firms are very kind and will send you the document along with a bill. Other firms won't do business with you unless you pay up first. Having a relationship with a firm makes all the difference. Our financial restructuring group uses the New Generation [109] database, for example, so I'm always on the phone with them asking for additional research.

The New Generation database?

New Generation is a bankruptcy data source. The firm is in Boston and they recently started to market their database to the general public. They put out a bankruptcy almanac each year that is one-of-a-kind.

How does the Internet tie in to your research?

I'm always on the Net. But for research professionals, the Internet didn't quite provoke a "gee-whiz" sentiment. It has merely become a different way to access the databases we used to access through dial-up systems. If we didn't have the Internet, we would still have access to all of our databases. So, to some degree, the Internet really hasn't changed matters except for adding another source to check. However, if I were a government documents specialist or a demographic researcher, the Internet would be manna from heaven, because the information of interest to those folks is on the Net these days, whereas it used to be very hard to get that type of material quickly.

Bruce, you've built on your traditional reference-type background and developed an expertise in M&A research. How did you learn about finance?

A lot of what I've learned has been on the job, under a fair amount of trial-by-fire type pressure. At the larger investment banks, you'll find a lot of analysts and associates who have MBAs but who have come over from other backgrounds and don't know anything about finance either. They have to start from scratch, too. But I did take the Series 7 course when I was at Merrill so that I could have a better understanding of the material I was researching. Taking the course helped me get into the minds of the professional staff. You do need to learn that stuff, you need to know when to say "that information's in the proxy statement."

What is that Series 7 course?

The Series 7 course prepares you for the National Association of Securities Dealers mandated licensing test for all brokers. You can't be in any position of selling or recommending securities without passing that test.

What else do you recommend to anybody who's interested in doing M&A research?

Read as much as you can. I cannot emphasize enough how important it is to read. I read *The Wall Street Journal* every day. I also recommend publications such as *Investment Dealers Digest* [82] and *Pensions and Investments* [116], because they discuss particular corporate finance issues and the metrics of valuation by industry. By reading these magazines, I learned the meaning of a high-conversion premium and the phrase "out of the money."

Why is it so important? Because you understand what you're researching, what you're talking about, and you're gaining credibility. It all links together. But I'm also not afraid to ask questions. When I read something I don't understand, I always save it, and then I ask someone to explain it to me.

That's one more way an information professional can add value. Well, you know what? We've been talking for an hour, and we should probably wrap this up.

It's been an hour? But we're just getting started!

Super Searcher Power Tips

➤ You have to rely on your smarts, figure out where that information might be published, or who you can call.

➤ Sometimes trade magazines and newspapers will make a passing reference to the terms of a deal that will not be found in the transaction databases.

➤ People in investment banking love information products that include detailed business descriptions, since that helps them more accurately pinpoint competitors.

➤ Buyer's guides are worth their weight in gold because they list hundreds of companies that relate in some aspect to a particular industry, and they are much more descriptive than D&B or S&P directories.

➤ I don't want to show a preference for Dialog over Dow Jones or Lexis-Nexis, but I rely on Dialog because its indexing is so good.

Appendix A:
Referenced Resources

1. **10-K Wizard**
   www.10Kwizard.com

2. **ABI Inform (Dialog File 15)**
   library.dialog.com/bluesheets/html/bl0015.html

3. **Acquisitions Monthly**
   www.sdponline.com/products/mergers.html

4. **Amazon.com**
   www.amazon.com

5. **American Lawyer**
   www.americanlawyer.com

6. **American Society for Information Science and Technology (ASIST)**
   www.asis.org

7. **American Society of Appraisers**
   www.appraisers.org

8. **American Society of Association Executives**
   www.asaenet.org

9. **AP Tech Resources**
   www.aptechresources.com/mergers.htm

10. **Asia Intelligence Wire**
    www.ftep.ft.com/solutions/all/all/aiwsrc.htm

11. **ASIST (see American Society for Information Science and Technology)**

12. **Asset Alternatives**
    www.assetnews.com

13. **Association for Corporate Growth**
    www.acg.org

14. **AutoTrack**
www.dbt.com

15. **Bankruptcydata.com**
www.bankruptcydata.com

16. **BIZCOMPS**
www.bizcomps.com

17. **Bloomberg**
www.bloomberg.com

18. **Business and Finance Division Bulletin (Special Libraries Association)**
www.sla.org/membership/divisions/bus.html

19. **Business and Industry (Dialog File 9)**
library.dialog.com/bluesheets/html/bl0009.html

20. **Business Dateline (Dialog File 635)**
library.dialog.com/bluesheets/html/bl0635.html

21. **Business Reference Guide**
www.businessbrokeragepress.com

22. **Business Valuations by Industry**
cgr.nvst.com/qscBVIbuy.asp

23. **Buslib-L**
To subscribe, send email to:
listserv@listserv.boiseset.edu
In message body type:
Subscribe buslib-l firstname lastname

24. **Buyouts**
buyouts.nvst.com/pBUYHome.asp

25. **Carson Group**
www.carsongroup.com or www.xls.com

26. **CDB Infotek (see ChoicePoint)**

27. **Capital Changes Reporter**
www.cch.com

28. **ChoicePoint**
www.cdb.com

29. **CNET Finance and Investing**
investor.cnet.com/

30. **CNET Tech News**
news.cnet.com/

31. **Compact Disclosure**
www.primark.com

32. **CommScan**
www.commscan.com

33. **Compustat**
www.compustat.com

34. **Computasoft Research**
research.computasoft.com

35. **CorpFin**
www.corpfin.com

36. **Corporate Counsel**
Executive Press
P.O. 21639
Concord CA 94521-0639
925-685-5111

37. **Corporate Governance Advisor**
www.aspenpub.com

38. **Corporate Growth Report**
cgr.nvst.com/qscCgr1.asp

39. **CT Advantage**
www.ctcorporation.com

40. **DailyStocks.com**
www.dailystocks.com

41. **Daily Deal**
www.thedailydeal.com

42. **Database (see EContent)**

43. **Data Downlink**
www.datadownlink.com

44. **Dialog Corporation**
www.dialog.com

45. **Disclosure**
www.disclosure.com

46. **DoneDeals**
www.nvst.com

47. **Dow Jones Interactive (See Factiva)**

48. **DRI**
www.dri.mcgraw-hill.com

49. **Dun & Bradstreet**
www.dnb.com

50. **EContent (formerly Database)**
www.ecmag.net

51. **EDGAR**
    edgar.sec.gov

52. **Encyclopedia of Associations**
    www.galegroup.com

53. **Encyclopedia of Business Information Sources**
    www.galegroup.com

54. **Factiva (formerly Dow Jones Interactive)**
    www.factiva.com

55. **FactSet**
    www.factset.com

56. **Financial News**
    www.financialnews.co.uk

57. **FIS Online (Moody's)**
    www.fisonline.com

58. **Flatiron Partners**
    www.flatironpartners.com

59. **FreeEDGAR**
    www.freeedgar.com

60. **Free Pint**
    www.freepint.com

61. **Global Access**
    www.disclosure.com

62. **Hoover's**
    www.hoovers.com

63. **IBA Market Database**
    www.instbusapp.org

64. **IncSpot**
    www.incspot.com

65. **The Industry Standard**
    www.thestandard.com

66. **Industry Week**
    www.industryweek.com

67. **Information Advisor**
    www.findsvp.com/publications/

68. **Information America**
    www.infoam.com

69. **Information Freeway Report**
    www.researchers.com (click Publication Catalog)

70. **Information Outlook**
www.informationoutlook.com

71. **Information Resources (IRI)**
www.infores.com

72. **Information Today**
www.infotoday.com/it/itnew.htm

73. **Information World Review**
www.iwr.co.uk/iwr

74. **InSite Pro**
www.insitepro.com

75. **Institute of Business Appraisers**
www.instbusapp.org

76. **Institutional Investor**
www.iimagazine.com

77. **International Business Brokers Association**
www.ibba.org

78. **International Mergers & Acquisitions Professionals (IMAP)**
www.imap.com

79. **InterNIC**
www.internic.net

80. **Intranets 2000**
www.intranets2000.com

81. **Investext**
www.investext.com

82. **Investment Dealers Digest**
www.sdponline.com/products/banking.html

83. **Investor Research and Responsibility Center**
www.store.irc.org

84. **IPO.com**
www.ipo.com

85. **IPO Financial**
www.ipofinancial.com

86. **John Wiley and Sons**
www.wiley.com

87. **Joint Venture Database**
www.tfsd.com/products/financial/default.asp

88. **Kagan and Associates**
www.kagan.com

89. **Kompass**
www.kompass.com

90. **Lexis-Nexis**
www.lexis-nexis.com

91. **LIVEDGAR**
www.gsionline.com

92. **Loan Pricing Corp.**
www.loanpricing.com

93. **M&A Daily**
www.madaily.com

94. **M&A Filings (Dialog File #548)**
library.dialog.com/bluesheets/html/bl0548.html

95. **Market Guide**
www.marketguide.com

96. **Merger Yearbook**
www.sdponline.com/products/mergers.html

97. **MergerMarket.com**
www.mergerMarket.com

98. **Mergers & Acquisitions**
www.sdponline.com/products/mergers.html

99. **Mergers and Acquisitions Sourcebook**
cgr.nvst.com/qscMas1.asp

100. **Mergers-R-Us**
www.mergers-r-us.com

101. **Mergerstat**
www.mergerstat.com

102. **Mergerstat Review**
www.mergerstat.com

103. **Million Dollar Directory**
www.dnbmdd.com

104. **Moneyzone.com**
www.moneyzone.com

105. **Moody's Company Data (see FIS Online)**

106. **National Association of Certified Valuation Analysts**
www.nacva.com

107. **National Association of Securities Dealers**
www.nasdr.com

108. **National Law Journal**
www.nlj.com

109. **New Generation**
www.turnarounds.com

110. **NewsEdge**
www.newsedge.com

111. **NVST.com**
www.nvst.com

112. **Official Company Filings in the European Union**
Book available from Sylvia James
da-james@11daymer.freeserve.co.uk.

113. **OneSource**
www.onesource.com

114. **Online**
www.onlineinc.com/onlinemag/index.html

115. **Online World**
www.onlineworld2000.com

116. **Pensions and Investments**
www.pionline.com

117. **PMD (see Portfolio Management Data)**

118. **Portal B**
www.portalb.com

119. **Portfolio Management Data (PMD)**
www.pmdzone.com

120. **Practitioner's Publishing Company**
www.ppcinfo.com

121. **Pratt's Stats (now Business Valuation Resources)**
www.bvresources.com

122. **PriceWaterhouseCoopers**
www.pwcglobal.com

123. **Profound**
www.profound.com

124. **PROMT (Dialog File 16)**
library.dialog.com/bluesheets/html/bl0016.html

125. **ProQuest**
www.proquest.com

126. **Quality Services Company**
     5290 Overpass Road, Suite 126
     Santa Barbara, CA 93111-2048
     805-964-7841

127. **Red Herring**
     www.redherring.com/mag

128. **SDC Platinum**
     www.tfsd.com/products/financial/default.asp

129. **Search Engine Showdown**
     www.notess.com or searchengineshowdown.com/

130. **Search Engine Watch**
     www.searchenginewatch.com

131. **Searcher**
     www.infotoday.com/searcher/default.htm

132. **SEC (see U.S. Securities and Exchange Commission (SEC))**

133. **SECnet (see Washington Service Bureau)**

134. **Securities Data Company (now Thomson Financial Securities Data)**

135. **SI: Special Issues**
     Contact: Trip Wyckoff
     9597 Jones Road #118
     Houston, TX 77076
     281-469-6004
     Triptx1@worldnett.att.net

136. **SLA (See Special Libraries Association)**

137. **SNL Securities**
     www.snl.com

138. **Society of Competitive Intelligence Professionals (SCIP)**
     www.scip.org

139. **Special Libraries Association (SLA)**
     www.sla.org

140. **Spectrum Business Resources**
     www.spectrumbusiness.com

141. **Standard and Poor's**
     www.standardandpoors.com

142. **Standard & Poor's Industry Surveys**
     www.advisorinsight.com

143. **Stern Stewart & Co.**
     www.sternstewart.com

144. **Stock Exchanges Worldwide Links**
www.weblink.com.au/html/wstock.html

145. **StreetEye**
www.streeteye.com

146. **TableBase**
www.rdsinc.com/TableBase/default.htm

147. **Thomas Register of American Manufacturers**
www.thomasregister.com

148. **Thomson Financial Securities Data (TFSD) [formerly SDC]**
www.tfsd.com

149. **Trade and Industry Database (Dialog File 148)**
library.dialog.com/bluesheets/html/bl0148.html

150. **U.K. Regulatory News Service**
www.londonstockexchange.com

151. **U.S. Industry and Trade Outlook**
www.ntis.gov/product/industry-trade.htm or www.ita.doc.gov/outlook

152. **U.S. Securities and Exchange Commission (SEC)**
www.sec.gov

153. **ValueLine**
www.valueline.com

154. **Venture Economics**
www.ventureeconomics.com

155. **VentureOne**
www.ventureone.com

156. **Vickers Stock Research**
www.argusgroup.com or www.xls.com

157. **The Wall Street Journal**
www.wsj.com

158. **Washington Service Bureau**
www.wsb.com

159. **Webmergers.com**
www.webmergers.com

160. **Westlaw**
www.westlaw.com

161. **Wiley (see John Wiley and Sons)**

162. **World M&A Network**
www.worldm-anetwork.com

163. **Worldwide M&A Database**
     www.tfsd.com/products/financial/default.asp

164. **Wright Research Center**
     profiles.wisi.com

165. **xls.com**
     www.xls.com

Appendix B:
Glossary of Terms

Definitions are based on Campbell R. Harvey's Hypertextual Finance Glossary (www.duke.edu/~charvey/Classes/wpg/glossary.htm), the Securities and Exchange Commission's Guide to Corporate Filings (www.sec.gov/edaux /forms.htm), and Investorwords.com (www.investorwords.com).

'33 Act. Original U.S. securities legislation requiring full disclosure of material facts in a registration statement preceding the offering of securities, and prohibiting false representations and other fraudulent activities.

'34 Act. The Securities Exchange Act of 1934 delegated responsibility for enforcement to the Securities and Exchange Commission (SEC).

8-K. A report of unscheduled material events or corporate changes deemed of importance to the shareholders or to the SEC. Unscheduled material events include changes in control, acquisition or disposition of assets; bankruptcy, changes in the company's accountant, resignation of directors, financial statements or exhibits, change of fiscal year, or some other event deemed material to the company.

10-K. A report that provides a comprehensive overview of the registrant. The report must be filed within 90 days after close of company's fiscal year. Some of the items contained in this report include a description of business, properties, legal proceedings, market for common stock, and the financial statements.

10-Q. The quarterly financial report filed by most companies with the SEC. Although unaudited, this document provides a continuing view of a company's financial position during the year. The 10-Q report must be filed forty-five days after close of fiscal year quarter.

13-D. A schedule filed with the SEC when an individual acquires five percent or more of a company's registered equity securities. The company owning those securities is required to file the form within ten days of the acquisition.

14D-1. The tender offer filed with the SEC and the target company. This document contains the acquirer's background and terms of the offer.

14D-9. The response to the tender offer (see **14D-1**). This document, filed with the SEC, indicates whether the offer is friendly or hostile.

Acquirer. A firm or individual that is acquiring all or part of a company.

Angel investor. A person who invests in start-up companies that are typically too small to require venture capital funding.

Annual report. Yearly record of a publicly held company's financial condition. It includes a description of the firm's operations as well as balance sheet, income statement, and cash flow statement information. SEC rules require that the annual report be distributed to all shareholders.

ASCII. A data transmission code that is used to represent textual data. Often referred to as *plain text* format.

Asset transaction. A type of transaction in which only the assets are sold to the buyer. All responsibilities for any liabilities rest with the seller. Any unknown future liability claims, such as environmental clean-up, will also rest with the seller. See **Stock transaction.**

Balance sheet. A summary of a company's assets, liabilities, and owners' equity. Also called the statement of financial condition.

Brick and mortar. A term used to describe the physical presence of a business, such as a storefront. The term is commonly used when comparing Internet businesses with traditional businesses.

Bridge loan. Interim financing of one sort or another used to solidify a position until more permanent financing is arranged. Bridge loans are generally short-term.

Business appraisal. See **Business valuation.**

Business broker. See **Business intermediary.**

Business intermediary. A person who is licensed to sell businesses. Generally a business broker or intermediary conducts smaller transactions than an investment banker in the buying and selling of businesses.

Business valuation. The field of appraising businesses as going concerns. Generally this refers to the appraisal of the equity of privately owned companies.

Comparable transactions. When a company is in the process of being sold, transactions in which similar companies were sold are used to help establish a reasonable sales price.

Control premium. Additional consideration that is paid by an investor over a marketable minority equity value in order to own a controlling interest in the common stock of a company.

Controlling interest. A controlling interest represents at minimum ownership of fifty percent of the outstanding votes plus one vote. The owner has the ability to effect changes in the overall business structure and to influence business policies.

Cross-border. International mergers and acquisitions between companies headquartered in different countries.

Deal price. See **Transaction value.**

Deal price/discretionary earnings. A multiple equal to the aggregate transaction value divided by the target company's earnings before interest, taxes, depreciation, and amortization, plus owner's compensation, and any non-operating expenses.

Deal price/EBIT. A multiple equal to the aggregate transaction value divided by the target company's earnings before interest and taxes.

Deal price/EBITDA. A multiple equal to the aggregate transaction value divided by the target company's earnings before interest, taxes, depreciation, and amortization.

Deal price/net sales. A multiple equal to the aggregate transaction value divided by the net sales of the target company. Net sales represents sales after consideration of returns and discounts.

Derivative instruments. Contracts such as options and futures whose price is derived from the price of the underlying financial asset.

Derivative security. A financial security, such as an option, or future, whose value is derived in part from the value and characteristics of another security, the underlying order.

Disclosure filings. A company's release of all information pertaining to its business activity regardless of how that information may influence investors. This information is filed with the SEC.

Divestment. A complete asset or investment disposition such as outright sale or liquidation.

Due diligence. In the process of an acquisition, the acquiring firm is often allowed to see the target firm's internal books. The acquiring firm does an internal audit. Due diligence also refers to the process of looking for publicly available data about the target to find out any information that might affect the acquisition. Offers are often made contingent upon the resolution of the due-diligence process.

EBIT. Earnings Before Interest and Taxes. Another term for operating income.

EBITDA. Earnings Before Interest, Taxes, Depreciation, and Amortization.

Equity. Ownership interest in a firm.

Equity price/cash flow. A multiple defined as the price of the stock divided by net income plus depreciation, depletion, and amortization.

Equity price/EBIT. A multiple defined as the price of the stock divided by earnings before interest and taxes.

Equity price/net income. A multiple defined as the price of the stock divided by income after taxes.

Equity price/net sales. A multiple defined as the price of the stock divided by sales after discounts and returns.

Fair market value. The amount at which property would change hands between a willing seller and a willing buyer when neither is acting under compulsion and when both have reasonable knowledge of the relevant facts.

Filing requirements. Required filings for public companies with the Securities and Exchange Commission. See **10-K, 10-Q,** etc. for descriptions of some required documents.

Five-percent owner. In a public company any shareholder owning or acquiring five percent or more of the company's registered equity securities must file a Schedule 13D with the Securities and Exchange Commission within 10 days of an acquisition event.

Fixed assets. Long-lived property owned by a firm that is used in the production of its income. Tangible fixed assets include real estate, plant, and equipment. Intangible fixed assets include patents, trademarks, and customer recognition.

Form 3. A form filed with the SEC that identifies the company's securities that are owned by officers, directors, and ten-percent shareholders.

Form 4. An amendment to Form 3 that announces changes in the securities holdings of officers, directors, and ten-percent shareholders.

Form 5. An annual filing with the SEC filed 45 days after the company's fiscal year end.

Fragmented industry. An industry characterized by many individual regional or local businesses and very few companies that are national in scope.

Goodwill. Excess of the purchase price over the fair market value of the net assets acquired under the purchase method of accounting.

Gross sales. A company's total invoice value of sales, before deducting for customer discounts, allowances, or returns.

Hits. In the process of selling a business, an investment bank will prepare a list of potential buyers. Companies on this list that have an interest in the selling company are "hits."

Hostile takeover. A takeover of a company by an acquiring company or raider against the wishes of current management and the board of directors.

Initial public offering (IPO). A company's first sale of stock to the public. Securities offered in an IPO are often, but not always, those of young, small companies seeking outside equity capital and a public market for their stock. Investors purchasing stock in IPOs generally must be prepared to accept very large risks for the possibility of large gains.

Joint venture. An agreement between two or more firms to undertake the same business strategy and plan of action.

Limited liability company (LLC). This type of business entity has one or more general partners. Generally, the partners are not personally liable for the debts, obligations or liabilities of the LLC. Properly formed LLCs will be treated as partnerships for federal and state tax purposes.

Liquidity discount. This discount represents a lower value on a stock or company due to lack of a ready market. The value base from which the discount is subtracted is the value of an entity or interest that is otherwise comparable but enjoys higher liquidity (readily converted into cash).

Listed company. This term indicates that a company's stock is traded on an exchange. Synonyms include *listed security* or *listed stock*.

Main Street. Merger and acquisition deals with a value of less than $1 million.

Middle market. Merger and acquisition deals under $100 million in transaction value. Sometimes this figure is revised lower, to $50 million.

Minority interest. An interest in a company that does not allow the owner to effect changes in the business structure. A minority interest is equal to less than fifty percent of the votes of the outstanding equity.

Multiples. A ratio, usually having a value greater than 1. These ratios (see **Deal price/net sales**, etc.) represent a value measure that can be applied to an earnings definition of a specific company, which are used to estimate value.

Net sales. A company's gross sales minus returns, discounts, and allowances.

North American Industry Classification System (NAICS). A system of classifying businesses numerically by type. NAICS was adopted in 1997. Its numerical categories are significantly more detailed than Standard Industrial Classification Codes.

Poison pill. Any tactic by a company designed to avoid a hostile takeover. One example is the issuance of preferred stock that gives shareholders the right to redeem their shares at a premium after the takeover.

Price/book. This multiple is equal to the price of the company's stock divided by its net book value.

Price/earnings. This multiple is equal to the price of the company's stock divided by its earnings, usually after tax.

Price/EBIT. This multiple is equal to the price of the company's stock divided by its earnings before interest and taxes.

Price/EBITDA. This multiple is equal to the price of the company's stock divided by its earnings before interest, taxes, depreciation, and amortization.

Private equity. Equity that is not traded on any exchange and has no ready market. See **Privately held.**

Privately held. A privately held company is one that is not traded on any exchange and has no ready market. Private investors hold all of the equity.

Prospecting. The process of looking for potential clients for aid in selling or buying a business, raising capital, or preparing an IPO. Investment banks generally maintain prospect lists of potential clients.

Prospectus. Generally, a descriptive document. In the case of a prospectus filed with the SEC, when a company offers its securities for sale the document contains basic and financial information about the company.

Proxy. A proxy statement provides official notification to designated classes of shareholders of matters to be brought to a vote at a shareholders meeting. Proxy votes might be solicited for a change in company officers or for many other matters.

Proxy fight. In a hostile takeover, an acquiring company tries to convince the target company's shareholders that their board of directors should be forced out in favor of a new board of directors.

Publicly traded. Stock that is traded on an exchange.

Registration statements. There are two main types of registration statements: "offering" registrations filed under the Securities Act of 1933, and "trading" registrations filed under the Securities Exchange Act of 1934.

Restructuring. The reorganization of a company's operations.

Rights agreements. Privilege granted to existing shareholders of a corporation to subscribe to shares of a new issue of common stock before it is offered to the public. Such a right, which normally has a life of two to four weeks, is freely transferable and entitles the holder to buy the new common stock below the public offering price.

Rules of thumb. Basic formulas used to estimate the value of a company. Generally, rules of thumb are overly simplistic because they do not take into account how unique operating characteristics may affect the valuation.

S-8. The registration form filed with the SEC for securities to be offered to employees under stock option and various other employee benefit plans.

Secretary of State. For any given U.S. state, the Secretary of State is generally the auditor of public accounts, chief elections officer, and manager of the state's records.

Section 16. Refers to Securities and Exchange Forms 3, 4, and 5.

Series 7 license. Anyone who sells any type of security products, except commodity futures, is required to take the General Securities Registered Representative examination in order to receive a Series 7 license.

Standard Industrial Classification (SIC) Code. A classification system developed by the U.S. government that assigns each industry a unique code. The SIC system has been replaced by the **NAICS** system. Prior to the implementation of NAICS, corporations used SIC codes to describe their operations on their federal tax forms. Currently, most business-related information sources allow their data to be organized by SIC code.

Stock split. An increase in the number of outstanding shares of a company's stock, such that proportionate equity of each shareholder remains the same. The market price per share drops proportionately. Usually done to make a stock with a very high per-share price more accessible to small investors. Requires approval from the board of directors and shareholders.

Stock transaction. A transaction in which the buyer acquires the outstanding shares of the company. The buyer assumes the assets and liabilities of the company as well as any exposure for unknown events such as environmental damage. See **Asset transaction.**

Source documents. Documents filed with the SEC.

Target. A firm that is the object of an acquisition by another firm or group of investors.

Tender offer. A general offer made publicly and directly to a firm's shareholders to buy their stock at a price well above the current market price.

Transaction value. The total value of the exchange between a buyer and a seller for the interest in a company. This includes all facets of the deal such as assumption of long-term liabilities, cash paid, employment agreements, etc.

Underwrite stock. The procedure used by an intermediary, typically an investment bank, that brings securities to market. The underwriter guarantees the company issuing the securities a specified offering price in the underwriting agreement.

Uniform Commercial Code (UCC). A set of laws regulating commercial transactions, especially ones involving the sale of goods and secured transactions.

Valuation. The process of determining the value of an asset or company.

Venture capital. Money from businesses and individuals that is invested in small businesses and start-up companies. Because venture capital is an investment made in the hopes of profitable returns, it is invested in companies that show great growth potential.

Wall Street. Merger and acquisition deals valued at $100 million or more. Compare **Main Street.**

Appendix C:
Bibliography

Bell, Steven J. "Revisiting M & A Research: Introducing a new player." *Database*, August-September 1997, Vol. 20, No. 4, pp. 76-82.

Bell, Steven J. "M & A Moves Abroad: Databases for researching cross-border deals." *Database*, November 1991, Vol. 14, No. 5, pp. 20-32.

Bell, Steven J. "Business students find leverage online: Searching the M & A files." *Online*, July 1988, Vol. 12, No. 4, pp. 58-62.

Halperin, Michael, and Steven J. Bell. *Research Guide to Corporate Acquisitions, Mergers and Other Restructuring.* New York: Greenwood Press, 1993.

Mercer, Z. Christopher, and Lisa Doble. "Pratt's Stats." *Valuation Strategies*, November/December 1997, pp. 47-48.

Pratt, Shannon P. "Finding and Using Comparative Private Business Sales Data." American Society of Appraisers International Appraisal Conference. Houston, Texas, June 23, 1997.

Research Guide 11: Mergers & Acquisitions. The Lippincott Library, Wharton School of Business, University of Pennsylvania. www.library. upenn.edu/lippincott/pubs/rguides.html.

"The Right Data for the Job." Institute of Business Appraisers 2000 National Conference. (Panel discussion regarding when to use the numerous sources of market data for various types of appraisal assignments.)

Rock, Milton L., et al. *The Mergers and Acquisitions Handbook.* 2nd edition. New York: McGraw Hill, 1994.

Tudor, Jan Davis. "M&A Transactions." *EContent*, October/November 1999, pp. 63-65.

Tudor, Jan Davis, and Karin Zamba. "Sources of M&A Data for Business Valuations: Print or Electronic?" *Special Libraries Association Business & Finance Division Bulletin,* No. 106, Fall 1997, pp. 19-24.

Wasserstein, Bruce. *Big Deal: 2000 and Beyond.* Revised edition. New York: Warner Books, 2000.

About the Author

Jan Davis Tudor is President of JT Research LLC, located in Portland, OR. With a Master's degree in Library and Information Studies from the University of California at Berkeley, Jan has more than ten years of research experience in academic and corporate libraries. In business for herself since 1997, Jan and her staff provide information relating to industries, companies, and mergers and acquisitions to business appraisers, financial analysts, and economists. She speaks frequently across the country to groups of business professionals on the effective use of the Internet as a research tool, and has given workshops in Argentina and Japan. Jan is a columnist for *EContent* and the *CPA Litigation Services Counselor* and a member of the Association of Independent Information Professionals (AIIP) and the Special Libraries Association (SLA).

Jan lives in Portland, OR, with her husband, Greg. Like most Oregonians, she enjoys spending time outdoors in activities such as hiking and kayaking.

Photo by David Torres

About the Editor

Reva Basch, executive editor of the Super Searchers series, is a writer, researcher, and consultant to the online industry. She is the author of the original Super Searcher books, *Secrets of the Super Searchers* and *Secrets of the Super Net Searchers*, as well as *Researching Online For Dummies* and *Electronic Information Delivery: Ensuring Quality and Value*. She has contributed numerous articles and columns to professional journals and the popular press, and has keynoted at conferences in Europe, Scandinavia, Australia, Canada, and the U.S.

A past president of the Association of Independent Information Professionals, she has a Master's in Library Science from the University of California at Berkeley and more than 20 years of experience in database and Internet research. Basch was Vice President and Director of Research at Information on Demand and has been president of her own company, Aubergine Information Services, since 1986.

Reva lives with her husband and cats on the northern California coast.

Index

More CyberAge Books
From Information Today, Inc.

Super Searchers on Wall Street
Top Investment Professionals Share Their Online Research Secrets
Amelia Kassel • Edited by Reva Basch

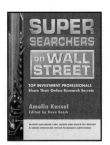

Through her probing interviews, Amelia Kassel reveals the online secrets of ten leading financial industry research experts. You'll learn how information professionals find and analyze market and industry data, as well as how online information is used by brokerages, stock exchanges, investment banks, and individual investors to make critical investment decisions. The Wall Street Super Searchers direct you to important sites and sources, illuminate the trends that are revolutionizing financial research, and help you use online research as part of a powerful investment strategy. As a reader bonus, a directory of top sites and sources is hyperlinked and periodically updated on the Web.

Softbound • ISBN 0-910965-42-0 • $24.95

Law of the Super Searchers
The Online Secrets of Top Legal Researchers
T.R. Halvorson • Edited by Reva Basch

In their own words, eight of the world's leading legal researchers explain how they use the Internet and online services to approach, analyze, and carry through a legal research project. In interviewing the experts, practicing attorney and online searcher T.R. Halvorson avoids the typical introductory approach to online research and focuses on topics critical to lawyers and legal research professionals: documenting the search, organizing a strategy, what to consider before logging on, efficient ways to build a search, and much more. *Law of the Super Searchers* offers fundamental strategies for legal researchers who need to take advantage of the wealth of information available online.

Softbound • ISBN 0-910965-34-X • $24.95

Super Searchers Do Business
The Online Secrets of Top Business Researchers
Mary Ellen Bates • Edited by Reva Basch

Super Searchers Do Business probes the minds of 11 leading researchers who use the Internet and online services to find critical business information. Through her in-depth interviews, Mary Ellen Bates—a business super searcher herself—gets the pros to reveal how they choose online sources, evaluate search results, and tackle the most challenging business research projects. Loaded with expert tips, techniques, and strategies, this is the first title in the exciting new "Super Searchers" series, edited by Reva Basch. If you do business research online, or plan to, let the Super Searchers be your guides.

Softbound• ISBN 0-910965-33-1 • $24.95

The Invisible Web
Uncovering Information Sources Search Engines Can't See

Chris Sherman and Gary Price

"A unique guide to the Web's hidden information resources... *The Invisible Web* is a must read for every serious online searcher."
—Danny Sullivan, editor, SearchEngineWatch.com

The "Invisible Web," which may account for 80% or more of the authoritative information available via the Internet, includes content-rich databases from governments, universities, libraries, associations, and businesses around the world. These valuable information repositories are appearing on Web servers at a staggering rate, but search engines can tell you little or nothing about the data they contain. In this new book, authors Chris Sherman and Gary Price share their strategies for successfully searching the Invisible Web. They reveal the top sites and sources for Invisible Web research, and offer tips, tools, techniques, and analysis that will let you pull needles out of haystacks every time. The companion Web directory provides linked access to hundreds of resources covered in the book.

Softbound • ISBN 0-910965-51-X • $29.95

Internet Business Intelligence
How to Build a Big Company System on a Small Company Budget

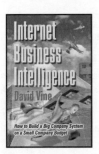

David Vine

According to author David Vine, business success in the competitive, global marketplace of the 21st century will depend on a firm's ability to use information effectively—and the most successful firms will be those that harness the Internet to create and maintain a powerful information edge. In *Internet Business Intelligence*, Vine explains how any company—large or small—can build a complete, low-cost Internet-based business intelligence system that really works. If you're fed up with Internet hype and wondering "where's the beef?," you'll appreciate this savvy, no-nonsense approach to using the Internet to solve everyday business problems and to stay one step ahead of the competition.

Softbound • ISBN 0-910965-35-8 • $29.95

Millennium Intelligence
Understanding & Conducting Competitive Intelligence in the Digital Age

Jerry P. Miller and the Business Intelligence Braintrust

With contributions from the world's leading business intelligence practitioners, here is a tremendously informative and practical look at the CI process, how it is changing, and how it can be managed effectively in the Digital Age. Loaded with case studies, tips, and techniques, chapters include: What Is Intelligence?; The Skills Needed to Execute Intelligence Effectively; Information Sources Used for Intelligence; The Legal and Ethical Aspects of Intelligence; Small Business Intelligence; Corporate Security and Intelligence; ... and much more!

Softbound • ISBN 0-910965-28-5 • $29.95